In case of loss, please return to:

_____

_____

_____

_____

As a reward: $_____

sacred roads

EXPLORING THE HISTORIC PATHS OF DISCIPLESHIP

EATHER ZEMPEL

Published by LifeWay Press®
© 2009 Heather Zempel
Second Printing June 2010

ISBN: 978-1-4158-6811-9
Item: P005233433

Dewey Decimal Classification Number: 234.2
Subject Heading: FAITH / SPIRITUAL LIFE / SPIRITUAL FORMATION—HISTORY OF
DOCTRINES

Printed in the United States of America.

Leadership and Adult Publishing
LifeWay Church Resources
One LifeWay Plaza
Nashville, Tennessee 37234-0175

We believe the Bible has God for its author; salvation for its end; and truth,
without any mixture of error, for its matter and that all Scripture is totally true
and trustworthy. The 2000 statement of *The Baptist Faith and Message* is our
doctrinal guideline.

Cover photography and design by Micah Kandros Design.

TABLE OF CONTENTS

MEET THE AUTHOR

My name is Heather Zempel, and I'm so glad you've picked up a copy of *Sacred Roads*. The ideas in this Bible study have been forming for a long time, and I've seen them fleshed out in practical ways in my role leading the discipleship efforts at National Community Church in Washington, D.C. Day in and day out, I try to provide leadership and vision for our small group ministry.

I grew up in Mobile, Alabama, and followed a circuitous route into full-time ministry. Having obtained bachelor's and master's degrees in biological engineering from Louisiana State University, I worked as an environmental engineer and as a policy consultant on energy and environment in the United States Senate before coming on staff at National Community Church.

My passion for engineering spiritual growth environments stems from my educational background. In fact, I frequently apply biological principles to the spiritual formation process. In doing so, I find myself continually seeking to understand and explain how different people learn and grow as followers of Christ. *Sacred Roads* is one result of those efforts, charting different historic paths of discipleship and demonstrating how they are all applicable for us as we grow in our relationship with Jesus.

I'm also a frequent speaker and writer on the topics of leadership, community, discipleship, and spiritual formation. I have the privilege of serving on the editorial board of *smallgroupexchange.com*, writing regularly for *smallgroups.com*, and frequently providing leadership training to small group leaders at other churches. I live on Capitol Hill with my husband Ryan.

You can find my ongoing blog regarding faith and discipleship at *heatherzempel.com*. Thanks again for exploring the nature, methods, and history of discipleship with me. Have fun on your journey of *Sacred Roads*.

dare to explore

Adventure?

Explore. Imagine. Experience. Discipline. Relate. Train. Receive. Care. Act. Inspire. Understand. Enlighten. Grow. Transform. These are words that describe the process of spiritual growth, components of a challenge passed down to us from the red letters of Scripture through the generations of long-gone Christ-followers. Though the word has grown stale and cold for many of us, this is the adventure of *discipleship*.

DISCIPLESHIP WITH JESUS WAS NEVER REDUCED TO A WORKBOOK OF QUESTIONS WITH OBVIOUS AND SIMPLISTIC ANSWERS. IT WAS RAW, ACTIVE, IN YOUR FACE.

Adventure is the right word for this process, because the pages of Scripture reveal anything but a dull life for the disciples. As far as we can tell, Jesus never herded His 12 Galilean buddies into a living room for an evening of cookies, Kool-Aid, and surface conversation, labeling it a "discipleship group." Discipleship with Jesus was never reduced to a workbook of questions with obvious and simplistic answers. It was raw, active, in your face. The dead were being raised, demons were flying out of people, and Pharisees were being smacked upside the head (metaphorically speaking, except for during Jesus' temple tantrum; then it might have been for real). And there was never a one-size-fits-all approach to anything.

In just one chapter in the Book of Luke, for instance, we observe Jesus' creative and unorthodox strategies. Luke 5 records Jesus interacting with people in various ways. He gave people like Peter life-changing experiences. He met people like the leper at the place of their deepest needs and then changed their physical circumstances. He valued personal time with His Father even when the ministry demands were at an all-time high. He questioned the teaching of the religious leaders and debated them on an intellectual level. And He invited people like Matthew into relationship with Him.

This chapter stands in stark contrast to the formulaic Pharisees who were committed to growing closer to God by following the rules they had been following for hundreds of years. They were too small-minded to see the bigger story that God was writing throughout history. Now Jesus didn't throw out the rules, but He did re-imagine, re-invent, and re-engineer them. He developed new methods and metaphors for what a growing relationship with God looked like and He implemented new pathways for discipleship. Experiences. Compassion. Personal discipline. Battle of the minds. Relationships. These were the sacred roads Jesus used to draw people into deepening intimacy with God.

SPIRITUAL CHORES

Here's my concern: our generation is failing to meet Jesus' challenge to become and make disciples because, in true Pharisee fashion, we have sought to follow a law. In doing so, we've reduced discipleship to a one-size-fits-all program of do's, don'ts, and meetings. We've replaced spiritual workouts with spiritual worksheets, and that has left our spiritual experience boring, stale, and predictable. In the past, at least for me, discipleship typically got reduced to a list of approved spiritual chores that supposedly would help me become more like Jesus and closer to God. And to be fair, the spiritual chores often did help me grow. But there were other experiences that weren't on the list that often led to more dramatic growth.

WHEN I BEGAN TO EXPLORE MY OWN HERITAGE AS A FOLLOWER OF CHRIST, I DISCOVERED SACRED ROADS FOR DISCIPLESHIP THAT COULD CATALYZE MY OWN SPIRITUAL GROWTH. At the youth retreat at Covenant College, I experienced the power of Christian community—the kind where you eat a bunch of PayDay candy bars, wash them down with Orange Crush, and then throw it all up in the bathroom. And your friends are there for you.

When I celebrated communion at Christ Anglican Church, I experienced the holiness of God and the mystery of His presence in a way that opened my eyes to a new dimension of His character. Digging for dinosaur bones in Drumheller, Canada, helped me understand the majesty and sovereignty of God more than any sermon or book I had ever read on the subject. Taking notes in Mrs. Waite's fourth grade Bible class gave me an appreciation for learning theology and for journaling my walk with Christ. Practicing for the children's Bible Drill Team developed within me a love for the Word of God and a desire to know it better. Reading about the life of John Wesley spurred me to grow in my faith more than any Sunday School lesson.

Is it possible that there are encounters with Jesus and opportunities for growth that occur outside the approved list of spiritual chores? The disciples were lucky enough to be a part of a grand adventure that took them all over the known world. For us, the adventure seems reduced to Sunday School literature, sermons, slides from the visiting missionary, and the occasional potluck.

There must be more . . .

HISTORICAL AMNESIA

I'm also concerned that we have not met the discipleship challenge because, like the Pharisees, we do not see the larger story that God is writing throughout history. Bruce Shelley, author of *Church History in Plain Language* begins his book, "Many Christians today suffer from historical amnesia."[1] That was my diagnosis. Historical amnesia. It was also the reason I failed to understand discipleship. I had neglected 2,000 years of experiments and discoveries. In ignorance, I did not realize the wealth of spiritual growth opportunities that the church had used throughout its history.

When I began to explore my own heritage as a follower of Christ, I discovered sacred roads for discipleship that could catalyze my own spiritual growth. Exploring the history of church in the Catacombs gave me a new understanding and appreciation for Christian community. Realizing that God was still at work between Constantine and the Reformation, I rescued some proverbial babies that most Protestants threw out with the bath water. I even conceded that the social gospel, no matter how theologically messed up it might have become, had some things to teach me about the heart of Jesus.

DARE TO EXPLORE

Over the next few pages, I want to take you on a pilgrimage. I want to explore our history as the people of God and search for discipleship discoveries that we might re-imagine and re-invent for the 21st century. We will zoom out to see the big picture of some of the major historical and cultural shifts within the church over the past 2,000 years and how those changes affected the way people approached following Christ. We will talk about the sacred roads the church used throughout history to help people learn about, grow closer to, and look more like Christ.

We'll also examine what the Bible says about each, knowing that our methods of spiritual formation must be rooted in the Word of God if they are to be legitimate and produce any sort of permanent and positive life change. We will explore the Old Testament, the life and teachings of Jesus, and the practice of the early church to find examples of each expression of discipleship.

After rooting our understanding of each sacred road of discipleship in Scripture, we'll talk about a variety of modern-day expressions for each. We'll broaden our understanding of discipleship and seek to incorporate new spiritual formation practices into daily life. But we will also be challenged to expose ourselves to other methods and expressions because every now and then, it's good to experience our faith in ways that are foreign or uncomfortable. That stretches us.

Ultimately, though, this study will only be worthwhile if it's practiced more than it's studied. Otherwise, we'll once again fall into the trap of replacing spiritual workouts with spiritual worksheets and reducing the discipleship adventure to a workbook. Consider this a travel guide that gives you ideas of where to explore instead of a travelogue that simply gives pictures of someone else's trip.

Let's begin our journey . . .

session one
Relational Discipleship

He ran down the long stairs on the south side of the building that had represented his faith for as long as he could remember. Though he loved the building, it was no longer where he found meaning, purpose, or even the presence of God. Instead, his focus had shifted from the building to the people there—particularly the ones, like him, who had believed in the message of Jesus. All their lives had been flipped upside down, and they were learning and growing together.

He thought that the word "together" might best represent his life right now. His fellow believers were the ones motivating his faith and changing his heart. They were taking care of one another and encouraging each other in the faith. They were praying and singing, eating and playing. All the while, they knew they were in the presence of Jesus. He found that his thoughts about others were turning into spontaneous prayers of blessing.

"Stephen!" He heard his name shouted from behind him. "Here's the daily ration." Timon handed him a bag filled with bread and fruits.

"Thanks, Timon. And my family will be joining you for evening meal and prayers tonight." The bread looked good today. Just a few days before, Stephen had been selected to help deliver food to the widows in their community.

Stephen turned the corner and ran into some of the leaders of the synagogue. While he had enjoyed their conversations in the past, he didn't want to get into another debate today. As he passed them, he heard a voice he didn't recognize shouting, "We heard him blaspheme Moses and even God!"

Stephen suddenly realized that this was not going to be just another day of religious debate.

Later that day, Stephen preached with boldness and authority, telling the story of God throughout their history and declaring Jesus as the Messiah. For this, he was stoned to death, becoming the first Christian martyr.

THE COACH'S OFFICE

The final bell of the day rang and students poured out of their classes, slung books in lockers, and headed out to the parking lot. As a student with the unfortunate distinction of being a teacher's kid, I was required to busy myself for an extra 30 minutes of my school day as I waited for my mom to discharge her remaining duties and pack up another night's worth of grading materials.

In my seventh grade year, the office of a teacher and coach named Barry Murphy became my favorite after-school hangout. I think I initially spent time with him because he knew a lot about the music I loved. (I refuse to list or even hint at who those artists might be for fear of losing all credibility before you even make it to the next page of this book. Let's just say that a few of them probably showed up on the cover of some 80s-era issues of a magazine called *CCM*.)

"We cared so much for you that we were pleased to share with you not only the gospel of God but also our own lives, because you had become dear to us" (1 Thessalonians 2:8).

Coach Murphy earned a few jewels in his crown over the next two years as he spent countless hours listening to me pontificate about life, God, and music. And through those talks, he patiently and enthusiastically encouraged me to pursue an authentic relationship with Jesus. My life had already been filled with dozens of Sunday School teachers, Vacation Bible School leaders, and camp counselors, but Barry stands out as one who made a significant and lasting impression on my life in a very vulnerable and formative season.

As I look back, it's difficult to remember specific lessons he taught me, but it was during those two years when I grew exponentially in my young relationship with Jesus. I started a daily quiet time and began to journal about what I was reading in the Bible. I don't think Barry was intentionally discipling me, and I wasn't intentionally seeking to be discipled. It was just the kind of spiritual growth that happens when life contacts life.

Following Christ is never a solo flight. We grow through shared circumstances, conversations, and hard questions as we dare to enter into the sphere of relational discipleship.

> **List three people who have made a significant difference in your life. Have you ever stopped to thank them for their contribution?**

GROWING IN FAITH THROUGH COMMUNITY

Author Julie Gorman said, "Community is not optional. We will not mature into the fullness God intends without it." The relational model of discipleship was the dominant approach to spiritual growth during the first few centuries of the church. Relational discipleship is predicated on the idea that we grow closer to Christ as we grow closer to one another. Spiritual growth happens when we actually live in community as the body of Christ and become the answer to His prayer that we would be "one."

Do you believe we won't mature in Christ without community? Why or why not?

Can you think of some times in your life when community and relationships played a specific and significant role in your spiritual growth? Describe the circumstances and how community changed you.

During the first few centuries of Christian history, community was the driving force of the church. In those days, the church wasn't considered a place, a building, or an event. It was a movement fueled by the experiences and missional hearts of people, and discipleship primarily happened through a vast and intricate network of relationships. That's the relational expression of discipleship—growing closer to Christ as we grow closer to one another.

BEING THE CHURCH

The first-century church was organic. There were no buildings, no Bibles, no Christian Life Centers, no stained glass—just people connected by a common experience and a common purpose. They all had the experience of a life-changing encounter with Jesus Christ and the purpose of sharing that experience with others. Discipleship grew out of those commonalities.

John 17 records Jesus' intercessory prayer for Himself and His followers just before His death. Among other things, Jesus prayed that His followers might be brought to complete unity, saying: "May they all be one, as You, Father, are in Me and I am in You" (v. 21).

"When we honestly ask ourselves which persons in our lives mean the most to us, we often find that it is those who, instead of giving much advice, solutions, or cures, have chosen rather to share our pain and touch our wounds with a gentle and tender hand."[3]
—Henri Nouwen

In *Water From a Deep Well*, Gerald Sittser describes the growth of the first-century church: "They did not use organized rallies, high-profile evangelists and big-budget programs to win recruits. If anything, Christians maintained a low profile to avoid public notice. The church thus attracted outsiders through natural networks of relationships." He continued, "The church became like family to aliens and outsiders who flocked to the cities." Peter Brown confirmed, "The appeal of Christianity still lay in its radical sense of community; it absorbed people because the individual could drop from a wide impersonal world into a miniature community."

Before followers of Christ were even referred to as "Christians," their gatherings were associated with the Greek word *ekklesia*, a word referring to a gathering of a group of people. That word was later translated into the word "church," which is now fraught with meanings and images of buildings, structures, and events that bear little resemblance to the original. Read every word of the New Testament. Not once do you see anyone "going to church." We never find Peter asking John, "Hey, can I catch a ride to church with you today?" Or Andrew asking, "Who wants to go fishing after church?"

They couldn't *go* to church because they *were* the church.

How does an understanding of the word *ekklesia* change your understanding of what the church is?

Do you find yourself *going* to church or *being* the church? List some differences between these two concepts.

When Jesus told Peter "On this rock I will build My church" (Matthew 16:18), He wasn't referring to a concrete slab or a structure of bricks and mortar. He was envisioning a building structured of the connections of

In order to dig out Greek meanings as you read Scripture, use a concordance, a Bible dictionary, and an interlinear Bible. Countless book options are available, but you can also find these tools on Web sites such as *lifeway.com/bible*, *biblestudytools.com*, *studylight.org*, and *bible.org*

Within one century of the death and resurrection of Jesus Christ, the gospel had spread throughout the entire known world and a church had been planted in most of the major cities of the Roman Empire. Without buildings, the New Testament, or denominational structures, the faith was passed from person to person.

people. It's a metaphor Peter would reference in his own writings many years later—"you yourselves, as living stones, are being built into a spiritual house" (1 Peter 2:5).

The church was a network of relationships. And spiritual growth did not happen through equipping classes or DVD curriculum; it happened as lives rubbed against other lives. Without church bylaws, committees, and other aspects of modern church life, early Christ-followers grew closer to Christ as they grew closer to one another and promoted "love and good works" (Hebrews 10:24). Christian character was built primarily through influence as opposed to instruction (remember how Paul said to imitate him in 1 Corinthians 4:16?), and spiritual truths were conveyed through the stories of the apostles and their letters to the churches.

RABBIS, CATACOMBS, AND LOVE FEASTS

The first church was mainly comprised of Jews who believed in Jesus as the Messiah, so discipleship was heavily influenced by the discipleship practices of Judaism—specifically, the rabbinical tradition. Rabbis were respected scholars and religious leaders who would invest their lives in a chosen number of pupils and allow them to accompany them on their faith journey. Students would sit at the feet of the rabbis and learn through the exchange of questions. Paul was a rabbi, and his training was evident in the way he pulled people into his life for one-on-one instruction and learning through shared experience.

The environments in which the early church met also influenced the type of discipleship that happened. The second chapter of Acts reveals that the early followers of Christ met in houses and shared meals. There were no platforms or pulpits. People didn't sit facing in one direction toward a single speaker. Instead, they faced one another as they gathered in living rooms, in the desert, at the graves of the martyrs, in the catacombs, and in other unlikely places. Justin Martyr said, "The Christians assemble wherever it is convenient, because their God is not, like the gods of the heathen, enclosed in space, but is invisibly present everywhere." Their faith experience did not occur during a two-hour window on a specific day of the week in a specific location. It saturated their everyday, walking-around lives.

Spiritual instruction happened through two primary means—the passing of apostolic letters and the sharing of the "love feast." Some of those letters were used so widely by the churches that they eventually became part of the canon of Scripture. Galatians, Ephesians,

An overwhelming 90 percent of young adults surveyed by LifeWay Research believe they can have a good relationship with God without being involved in church. This is just one reason relational discipleship is so important.

In Messianic Synagogues, like Tikvat David outside of Atlanta, this same rabbinical tradition of communal discipleship is still practiced. Tikvat David's mission statement reads, "Our synagogue is about three simple things: Torah, Messiah, and Community.... Forming a redemptive, healing community is our vision." (See *hopeofdavid.org/Tikvat_David*.)

Justin Martyr was an early Christian apologist who lived during the second century A.D. Tradition holds that he was martyred under the emperor Marcus Aurelius.

Corinthians, Colossians—they aren't just funny names. They were letters written to specific people or groups of people at a specific time for a specific reason. We recognize them now as books written under the inspiration of the Holy Spirit, but at the time, they were simply letters written to friends that went viral.

The love feast was the observance of Communion, or the Lord's Supper, within the context of a much larger shared meal. In the early church, Communion did not consist of a small stale wafer and a tiny plastic glass of grape juice. Communion was observed as part of a larger feast shared by the community. The "love feast" is clearly referenced in Jude 1:12, and is implied in 2 Peter 2:13, 1 Corinthians 11:17-34, and Acts 6:1-3. The purpose of the meal was to remember Jesus' sacrifice, encourage His followers, and experience God's love.

Spiritual growth happened in ancient living rooms and around tables.

Different traditions refer to Communion by different names. It is also called the Eucharist and the Lord's Supper. While different theological traditions argue over the sacramental versus symbolic nature of the practice, it is agreed that the observance of Communion is an opportunity to celebrate Christ's sacrifice, express your thankfulness for your salvation, declare your allegiance to Christ, and identify yourself with the body of Christ.

PICTURES OF THE CHURCH

The biblical text is replete with examples of relational discipleship. Consider some of the metaphors used by the New Testament writers to describe the church:

The Church is a Body
"Now you are the body of Christ, and individual members of it" (1 Corinthians 12:27).

The Church is a Family
"So then you are no longer foreigners and strangers, but fellow citizens with the saints, and members of God's household" (Ephesians 2:19).

The Church is the Bride of Christ
"Then one of the seven angels, who had held the seven bowls filled with the seven last plagues, came and spoke with me: 'Come, I will show you the bride, the wife of the Lamb'" (Revelation 21:9).

> As you think about the church as a body, a family, and the bride of Christ, which metaphor resonates with you the most? Why?

If the church is the body of Christ, what body part do you fulfill? Why?

RELATIONAL DISCIPLESHIP IN THE OLD TESTAMENT

There are numerous examples of relational discipleship in the Old Testament. A reluctant leader passes the baton of leadership to a young protégé just when the promised land comes into sight. An aging prophet throws his cloak around a farmer, and the farmer leaves behind his plow to follow him. A young widow clings to her mother-in-law and follows her to a strange land and people where she ultimately finds redemption. Each of these examples shows us the value relationships can have in influencing our walks with God.

Moses and Joshua

When I look at the relationship between Moses and Joshua, I think of the words "training" and "opportunity." Joshua first appears on the pages of Scripture in Exodus 17 when Moses asked him to lead the army of Israel against the Amalekites. Moses stood at the top of the hill raising the staff of God while Joshua led the men to fight. In Exodus 24, Joshua became known as "Moses' assistant."

For 40 years, Joshua stood by Moses' side, and they experienced life and leadership together. Joshua lingered at the tent of meeting in hopes of experiencing the presence of God. He was dispatched as a spy into the promised land. In Numbers 27, Moses showed Joshua the land that had been promised to them, he laid his hands on Joshua, and proclaimed him the new leader of Israel. Moses encouraged him publicly in Deuteronomy 31:7:

"Moses then summoned Joshua and said to him in the sight of all Israel, 'Be strong and courageous, for you will go with this people into the land the LORD swore to give to their fathers. You will enable them to take possession of it.'"

When the baton of leadership was passed from Moses to Joshua, it happened seamlessly and the people of Israel immediately recognized their new leader. Under Joshua's leadership, the Israelites began their conquest of the promised land.

"For a community to be whole and healthy, it must be based on people's love and concern for each other."
—Millard Fuller, founder of Habitat for Humanity

Though he led the people of God through the desert for 40 years, Moses was forbidden from actually entering the Promised Land because of his disobedience recorded in Numbers 20.

Joshua's military campaign is still studied in U.S. and Israeli war colleges.

Describe a time when someone trained you to do a job that they were doing. What did they do well? What did they not do well?

What's the value in a relationship like that for your spiritual journey?

Some of Elisha's best-known miracles include the parting of the Jordan River (2 Kings 2:13-14), raising the Shunammite woman's son from the dead (2 Kings 4:8-37), and the healing of Naaman (2 Kings 5).

Elijah and Elisha
Elijah was a prophet in Israel during the reign of some pretty nasty people. In 1 Kings 19:19, he walked up to a farmer named Elisha, threw his cloak over him, and walked away. Elisha interpreted that as an invitation to become the prophet's apprentice, so he killed his oxen, burned his plow, and began his leadership training by following Elijah the best he could. Scripture does not record any miracles performed by Elisha until the next book, in 2 Kings 2. In Elijah's last moments of his life on earth, Elisha refused to leave him behind. Clinging to him until the very last moments of life, Elisha made one final request: "Please, let there be a double portion of your spirit on me" (2 Kings 2:9).

Elisha is a great example of a person who followed well. Instead of pushing his own agenda, he quietly and faithfully assisted a leader until the end of his mission. His reward was a leadership gift that surpassed that of his mentor. Depending on the translation, Scripture records around 14 miracles performed by Elijah and about 28 miracles performed by Elisha. Looks like a double portion to me.

What are some characteristics of a good follower?

Is there anyone in your life right now God wants you to faithfully follow? If so, what are three practical things you can do to support that person?

Naomi and Ruth

We typically think of discipleship as a one-way relationship, often as an older person investing their wisdom and experience into a younger person. But the Book of Ruth demonstrates the two-way power of spiritual friendship. Naomi, an Israelite, lost her husband and both sons within the first five verses of the book. One daughter-in-law, a Moabite woman named Ruth, clung to Naomi and promised to remain a part of her life. Her faithfulness to her mother-in-law was rewarded later in the book when Naomi set Ruth up on a date with Boaz, the owner of a nearby barley field. As it turned out, Boaz was a close relative of Naomi's late husband, and as "kinsman redeemer," he lined up to marry Ruth. And the influence of this spiritual friendship didn't end there. Ruth would become the great-grandmother of King David and be listed in the genealogy of Jesus.

> **Scan through the Book of Ruth. How did Naomi help Ruth on her spiritual journey? How did Ruth help Naomi on her spiritual journey?**

> **How have you seen this two-way relationship work out in your own life?**

Naomi was so depressed after losing her husband and two sons that she changed her name to "Mara," which means bitter. That's not exactly an easy person to follow.

Ruth has a great back-story. Boaz, who became Ruth's husband, was the son of Rahab. Rahab was another non-Jewish woman and a former prostitute. Yet she was commended in Hebrews 11 for the faith she displayed when she protected the Jewish spies who had been sent by Joshua years earlier. You can read Rahab's story in Joshua 2.

RELATIONAL DISCIPLESHIP IN THE LIFE OF CHRIST

While Jesus implemented many different styles of discipleship in His ministry, the idea of relational discipleship was core to His strategy. He selected 12 men to "be with Him" (Mark 3:14).

Jesus' passion for relationships was also reflected in His prayers. In every Gospel, we read of Jesus' prayer in the garden of Gethsemane. But John showed us more of the scene in John 17. For 12 verses, Jesus prayed for His direct disciples, but in verse 20, He switched gears and prayed for a larger group:

"I pray not only for these, but also for those who believe in Me through their message. May they all be one, as You, Father, are in Me and I am in You. May they also be one in Us, so the world may believe You sent Me. I have given them the glory You have given Me. May they be one as We are one. I am in them and You are in Me. May they be made completely one, so the world may know You have sent Me and have loved them as You have loved Me" (vv. 20-23).

Moments before Jesus' betrayal, He prayed that His future followers would build a tight community that would reflect the community of the Trinity. Just as the members of the Trinity exhibit unique attributes of the Godhead yet walk in inseparable unity, so Christ desired His followers to live in community with one another.

And that's not all. In John 13:34-35, Jesus saw future evangelistic efforts hinging on the development of community:

"I give you a new commandment: love one another. Just as I have loved you, you must also love one another. By this all people will know that you are My disciples, if you have love for one another."

> **If people will know that we are followers of Christ because of our love for one another, then how easily could someone accuse you of being a Christian?**

> **What is one practical thing you can do to show love to another Christ-follower this week?**

The Master Plan of Evangelism by Robert Coleman is an incredibly helpful book about Jesus' approach to discipleship. Coleman argues that Jesus had an increasingly deep relationship of discipleship as people got closer to Him. He taught the crowds, but He discipled the Twelve, and He mentored only three—Peter, James, and John.

If you were organizing a group of people to change the world, would you have made choices similar to Jesus'? In *Twelve Ordinary Men,* John MacArthur examines the regular guys turned disciples who flipped the world upside down with the gospel.

RELATIONAL DISCIPLESHIP IN THE NEW TESTAMENT

The Book of Acts opens with a flurry of activity—Jesus giving His final commands, a new apostle being chosen, the believers praying, the Holy Spirit descending, and 3,000 people being baptized in one day. Then, Luke takes a break from the action, the camera pans back, and he gives us a picture of the early church:

"And they devoted themselves to the apostles' teaching, to fellowship, to the breaking of bread, and to prayers. Then fear came over everyone, and many wonders and signs were being performed through the apostles. Now all the believers were together and had everything in common. So they sold their possessions and property and distributed the proceeds to all, as anyone had a need. And every day they devoted themselves to meeting together in the temple complex, and broke bread from house to house. They ate their food with gladness and simplicity of heart, praising God and having favor with all the people. And every day the Lord added to them those who were being saved" (Acts 2:42-47).

The early believers were devoted to God's Word, to each other, to communion, and to prayer. They were "together" and "had everything in common." They took care of one another and threw dinner parties at each others' houses. And the church grew. Disciples were made.

I would submit the primary reason for growth was not the result of an evangelistic crusade or a personal evangelism effort. I think the church grew because the community was contagious. In his book, *Theology for the Community of God*, Stanley Grenz argues that God can be seen in the community of His followers: "Each person can be related to the image of God only within the context of life in community with others. Only in fellowship with others can we show forth what God is like, for God is the community of love." That seems to echo Jesus' prayer in John 17:21:

"May they all be one, as You, Father, are in Me and I am in You. May they also be one in Us, so the world may believe You sent Me."

The relational form of discipleship is most clearly seen in Paul's relationships. Think for a second about all the people Paul lived alongside of and the people who believed in him enough to see him become a mature disciple. Ananias risked his life to help Paul take his first steps into a relationship with Christ. Barnabas risked his reputation by standing up for Paul and vouching for his conversion and his character before the believers. Paul always had traveling buddies on his missionary journeys—Barnabas, Silas, Luke, and John Mark. While Paul

Luke wrote the Book of Luke and the Book of Acts. In each effort, he was concerned with the logical, accurate reporting of the facts of the life of Jesus and the spread of Christianity. His systematic approach to writing fits his background as a physician.

Justin Martyr wrote, "We who once took most pleasure in the means of increasing our wealth and property now bring what we have into a common fund and share with everyone in need."[8]

was clearly an acclaimed intellectual and an excellent communicator, his greatest legacy was relational—in the letters he wrote (which make up two-thirds of the New Testament) and the young pastors he trained (Timothy and Titus). Paul's exhortation to Timothy in 2 Timothy 2:2 sums up his discipleship strategy:

"And what you have heard from me in the presence of many witnesses, commit to faithful men who will be able to teach others also."

Because people have been diligent in following this command for 2,000 years, we are still reading Paul's words and worshiping Jesus today. In short, without biblical community and relational discipleship, we might not have known that Paul even existed.

What faithful people have passed the teachings of Jesus to you? What faithful people are you passing the teachings of Jesus to?

List three truths you have learned about Jesus that you could share with someone who is new in faith.

Thessalonica was a cosmopolitan city located on the route connecting the Roman Empire to Egypt and North Africa. You can read about the tumultuous beginning to the church, including mob violence and a night escape, in Acts 17.

Paul told the church at Thessalonica, "We cared so much for you that we were pleased to share with you not only the gospel of God but also our own lives, because you had become dear to us" (1 Thessalonians 2:8). The gospel isn't just about an intellectual passing of beliefs—it's about shared lives. There are 58 commands in Scripture that we cannot obey outside the context of relationships with other people. They are the "one another" commands—confess to one another, pray for one another, share each others' burdens, encourage one another, honor one another, serve one another, offer hospitality to one another, and on and on. These are spiritual disciplines that shape your character to reflect Christ, but they can only be practiced within the context of life in community with others.

Find five "one another" commands in Scripture. List one practical thing you will do this week to obey each of those commands.

PUTTING IT INTO PRACTICE

How can we apply relational discipleship in our lives today? The possibilities are endless, but let's look at three: small groups, accountability teams, and one-on-one mentoring.

SMALL GROUPS

If you're reading this book, then you're likely working through it in a small group of other Christ-followers. Whether it's a Sunday School class, a college fellowship group, or a weeknight home group, small groups consist of people who commit to one another for an agreed-upon period of time for the purpose of practicing relational discipleship. Julie Gorman said, "The purpose of a small group is not meetings but maturity."

Small groups are, by their very nature, relational—their purpose should be to connect people with one another and connect people with God. But much more than a club or just a time to hang out, small groups have at their end the purpose of spurring each participant on to a closer walk with Christ.

If you're not already in a small group, consider the following:

- Find three or four other people who are willing to meet together regularly for the purpose of reading and implementing this study.
- Consider signing a covenant together that outlines the goals— when you will meet, how often you will meet, what you will study, and what the expectations of group participants will be.
- Meet together regularly.
- Pray with one another and for one another.

Julie Gorman's *Community That Is Christian* is a helpful guide, marking out the key characteristics of Christian relationships and providing practical insight in the development of those relationships.

For examples of group covenants, check out the templates from two churches: Southeast Christian Church (*simplesmallgroups. net*) and North Point Community Church (*nsidegrouplife.com*). You can also find an example at *threadsmedia. com/covenant.*

Has your experience with small groups been more about developing community or spiritual growth? Can you accomplish both? Why or why not?

How can small groups help you grow in your faith?

Are there any areas of spiritual growth that might be difficult to address in a small group setting? Why?

ACCOUNTABILITY TEAMS

C. S. Lewis said, "We are born helpless. . . . We need others physically, emotionally, intellectually; we need them if we are to know anything, even ourselves." Other people see what we don't see, and we need people in our lives who are willing to educate us about ourselves in order that we might grow completely into the person God created us to be.

"The prayer of faith will save the sick person, and the Lord will raise him up; and if he has committed sins, he will be forgiven. Therefore, confess your sins to one another and pray for one another, so that you may be healed. The intense prayer of the righteous is very powerful" (James 5:15-16).

Who loves you but loves God more? Who loves you but loves the person God created you to be more? Who isn't afraid to ask the hard questions, to challenge you, to get you back on track?

James 5:16 encourages us to confess our sins to each other, but we are so individualized in our approach to faith that we have missed out on the healing power of confession. When we confess our sins to God, we receive forgiveness. When we confess our sins to one another, we receive healing. We receive the affirmation that comes from a physical, flesh and blood member of the body of Christ saying to us the words of Jesus to the woman accused of being in adultery: "Neither do I condemn you," said Jesus. "Go, and from now on do not sin any more" (John 8:11). There is a freedom that comes in confession.

Confession occurs best within the context of a small group of people who are committed to helping one another become all that God created them to be. It's a smaller group than the small group;

accountability teams typically consist of three to four people. Here are some tips for finding accountability partners:

- Enlist one, two, or three friends who are willing to meet regularly for the purpose of spurring one another on in your spiritual journeys. Make sure these are people who love you and will honor confidentiality.
- Give each other permission to ask about anything in your lives at any time.
- Have each person share two or three questions they need to be asked regularly (e.g., How is your prayer life? What did you learn in Bible reading this week? Did you look at anything on the television or Internet that you shouldn't have? Are you taking care of your health?, etc.) The questions will be as unique as you are and should pertain specifically to a growth area you want to pursue or a potential sinful habit you want to break.
- Decide on a stable time and place for meeting.
- Make sure the conversation stays positive. The purpose of an accountability group is not to wallow in sin, but to encourage one another to grow.
- Pray with and for one another.
- Start your accountability experiment with a specific time period. At the end of the agreed-upon time, assess the helpfulness of the process and elect to continue or stop meeting.

Describe a time when you confessed to another person. How did you feel before confessing? How did you feel after?

How would you like someone to respond if you confessed something to them?

John Wesley was a huge believer in accountability teams. In his system, each team asked each other a series of questions including:
- Do you desire to be told your faults?
- What known sins have you committed since our last meeting?
- What temptations have you met with?

Listen to the audio segment called "Experimenting with Relational Discipleship" this week. Your group leader will send it to you via e-mail, or you can download it at *threadsmedia.com/sacredroads*. These audio recordings are designed to help you connect with different expressions of discipleship.

ONE-ON-ONE MENTORING

Edgar Guest said, "I'd rather see a sermon than hear one any day. I'd rather one would walk with me than merely tell the way."   For too long, we have practiced travel agent discipleship in the church. Travel agents sit behind a desk, in the comfort of their offices, telling people where to go, how to get there, and what to do once they're there. Armed with colorful brochures, they attempt to impart great knowledge about a place they may or may not have ever explored themselves. We need more tour guides—people who are willing to strap on their hiking boots, go on the journey with us, and interpret what we are experiencing along the way.

Practicing one-on-one mentoring is like enlisting a tour guide. It's the kind of relational discipleship that we see in the friendships of Moses and Joshua, Elijah and Elisha, and Paul and Timothy. While it's typically viewed as an older person imparting their wisdom and experience to a younger person, mentoring does not have to be inter-generational. Rather, it's about befriending someone who has walked a particular road a little bit longer than you have. I've been mentored by people much older than me, and I've been mentored by people much younger than me. Here are some steps to developing a mentoring relationship:

- Make a list of things you would like to learn.
- Make a list of people who excel in those areas.
- Ask those people for one hour over a cup of coffee. Don't start by asking someone to mentor you. This can feel like an overwhelming task and responsibility for some people. And I've found that the best mentors typically respond that they have nothing to offer.
- If the coffee hour goes well, ask the person if they would be willing to meet with you again sometime.
- Know what you want. Be specific about the purpose of your meeting with them and what you hope to gain.

Here's a trick I've learned for being mentored by very busy people—get involved in something they are doing. Are they leading a small group? Join it. Are they leading a mission trip? Sign up. Do they need volunteers on a team they oversee? Get on board. Find a way to bless them and become a help to their ministry rather than a drain on it.

Make a list of three people you would like to and could feasibly spend one hour with.

Make a list of three people who would benefit from one hour of your time.

Listen to "Let Us Love and Sing and Wonder" by Laura Taylor from the *Sacred Roads* playlist. Your group leader can e-mail you the whole playlist, or you can download it at *threadsmedia.com/sacredroads*.

Life Together by Dietrich Bonhoeffer remains the definitive work on the nature of Christian community. Since it was first published, this short book has played a major role in the development of what life together in Christ is all about.

What separates this method of relational discipleship from the others listed? What's appealing about it to you?

CHANGE A LIFE

The three Synoptic Gospels (Matthew, Mark, and Luke) spotlight the healing of a leper or the casting out of a demon as Jesus' opening miracle. In that culture, those were big, loud, bombastic, and in that particular theological environment, hell-blasting miracles. But John? Well, he went a different direction in his Gospel. He chose to record the start of Jesus' ministry with the account of water changing to wine.

Don't get me wrong—that's definitely a cool miracle. But when you think about it in terms of eternal significance, it's pretty mundane. This incident doesn't seem to have much of an impact other than to keep the party going. It doesn't change the trajectory of a person's life. It doesn't reverse a curse or heal a lifelong debilitating disease.

What was Jesus doing here?

He was simply preserving a guy's dignity.

Jesus was invited to this wedding, which means He must have known the bride or the groom or most likely both. The wine started running low, a potentially humiliating thing for a party host in that culture, so Jesus came in to rescue a buddy in need.

While many of Jesus' miracles corrected people's physical limitations, it seems He had another goal in mind at times. Jesus was concerned with people's standing within their communities. Sometimes the greatest thing we can do is not related to *what* we can change in life but *whose* life we can change. We grow closer to Christ as we seek to invest in the lives of others. And we grow closer to Christ as we grow closer to one another.

Read these healing accounts in Matthew 4:23-25, Mark 1:21-28, Luke 4:31-37, and John 2:1-11.

Watch a modern film depicting what being on a team is all about—maybe *Miracle* or *Hoosiers*. Is there anything you can learn from these movies about what life in community is all about?

ANOTHER VOICE—ANOTHER ERA
JOHN WESLEY (1703–1791)

John Wesley was an Anglican minister who dared to take the preaching of the Scriptures outside the four walls of the church building and into the open air. While his sermons and writings are still with us, his greatest influence came from his focus on small groups and one-on-one discipleship. Recognizing that his legacy was dependent not only on his gifts and abilities, but also on the gifts and abilities of those he discipled, Wesley organized his followers into groups called "class meetings." At each meeting, participants shared their answers to a series of questions.

Wesley also invested significant time and energy in the development of young preachers. Even today, you can visit the chapel he built at Bristol and see the glass window above the sanctuary from which he would watch his young emerging ministers preach. After they preached, he would meet with each of them and evaluate their progress. More than 200 years later, we see the powerful results of relational discipleship. Wesley's movement brought us the United Methodist Church, the Methodist Church of Great Britain, the African Methodist Episcopal Church, and the Wesleyan Church, representing millions of Christ-followers today.

TRY IT OUT

Memorize James 5:16: *"Therefore, confess your sins to one another and pray for one another, so that you may be healed."*

Contact a few trusted friends about forming an accountability team. As you do, make a list of questions you need to be asked every week. Here are a few of John Wesley's questions to get you started:

- *Am I consciously or unconsciously creating the impression that I am a better person than I really am? In other words, am I a hypocrite?*
- *Am I honest in all my acts and words, or do I exaggerate?*
- *Do I confidentially pass on what was told to me in confidence?*
- *Can I be trusted?*
- *Am I a slave to dress, friends, work, or habits?*
- *Am I self-conscious, self-pitying, or self-justifying?*
- *Did the Bible live in me today?*
- *Do I give God time to speak to me everyday?*
- *Am I enjoying prayer?*
- *When did I last speak to someone else of my faith?*
- *Do I pray about the money I spend?*

session two
Experiential Discipleship

She rubbed her eyes slowly and deeply, hoping to wipe the headache away from her sleep-deprived body. For some reason, that triggered the pain in her feet. Actually, the pain had been there for days, but it had become unnoticed—until now. The blisters had healed during her stay in the city, but the muscles continued to spasm occasionally. For a moment, she thought about taking a seat on a nearby rock, but she decided the physical pain was an outward expression of her spiritual journey. In honor of her Savior, she would stand.

It had been several months and several hundred miles since she left her sisters at the convent in Galicia, but the journey facing her now was the most important one. The journey she would make over the next 48 hours was the reason she had traveled from the lush gardens of home and crossed the coastline of the Mediterranean to this ancient city. Year after year, the residents of this city and pilgrims from afar followed this same ritual, walked the same route, and prayed the same prayers.

The priest gathered the crowd. She looked around, trying to take it all in. This was the very grotto in which Jesus Himself met with His disciples on the night before the tragic event took place. For five hours, the priest led them in song, read Scripture passages, and prayed.

It was then that she took note of the multitude of people, their eyes revealing the exhaustion and hunger they were feeling from the fatigue of vigils and daily fasts. The mountain seemed higher going down than it had coming up. For the first time in her life, she felt like she was truly experiencing the agony of her Savior, and she understood more fully the sacrifice He expected when He instructed His disciples to take up their crosses.

Egeria was a Spanish woman, believed to be a nun, who made a series of pilgrimages to religious sites during the late fourth century. Her diaries, which record her adventures and personal reflections, have been preserved in her book, Itinerarium Egeriae.

NEAR DEATH EXPERIENCE

There were mixed reactions as we stepped into the ancient Crusader church, a structure unlike anything many of us had ever experienced. Incense filled the massive space. "It smells like Raid in here," observed my new friend from Texas. I wasn't sure whether to react with laughter, embarrassment, or horror. He was right, but wasn't this holy ground? After all, it was supposedly the place where Christ was crucified. Regardless of how foreign it seemed to some of us, the Church of the Holy Sepulcher seemed to require an attitude of reverence. I ascended the ancient stairs to the upper level of the church with a mixture of Protestant cynicism, insatiable curiosity, and great anticipation. If Constantine was correct, I was scaling the side of Golgotha, as Jesus had done 2,000 years earlier.

When I arrived at the top of the second level, I was overwhelmed with visual elements. Above us hung an image of Christ on the cross with two angels looking on. Incense candles were too numerous to count and too odorous to inhale, and ornate candelabras dropped from the ceiling. The entire floor was encased in glass. Beneath it was rock. There was an altar in the middle of the room and a picture of Christ beneath it. Underneath the altar was enough crawl space for one person to kneel before the picture of Christ and reach through a small hole in the glass to touch the rock below.

I titled my journal that day "Near Death Experience" and wrote the following:

"In the afternoon, we visited the Church of the Sepulcher (or Church of the Resurrection), which was built over the most likely site of the crucifixion and resurrection. Several denominations have a presence in the Church, but the Greek Orthodox tradition is very strong. Lots of incense. As we walked in, Adam said, 'It smells like Raid in here.' I like incense but I began to agree with him after awhile. In one chapel, you can approach the altar and reach through a hole to touch the rock of Golgotha. Only one person can approach the rock at a time, so it's a one-on-one encounter with Jesus. As I knelt there, I realized I was having a 'near death experience.' That rock should be the place of my death—but Jesus took it for me. As I meditated further, I remembered that we actually are called to die daily, so that Christ may live and be formed in us. The time at the rock of Golgotha was powerful. I couldn't stop saying 'Thank you so much.' I don't know that I have ever felt that thankful for Christ's sacrifice."

One minute changed my life. I felt like I had been born again . . . again.

There are two locations in Jerusalem which experts claim to be the place where Jesus was crucified, buried, and resurrected. One is the ancient Crusader site, the Church of the Holy Sepulcher. The other is the Garden Tomb located just outside the walls of the Old City.

Seven different Christian denominations have a presence in the Church of the Holy Sepulcher—Eastern Orthodox, Armenian Apostolic, Roman Catholic, Greek Orthodox, Coptic Orthodox, Ethiopian Orthodox, and Syriac Orthodox. Because the denominations cannot agree on who should be the primary custodian, a Muslim family has held the keys to the church since 1192. (That's not a misprint. Not 1992. 1192.) Twice daily, a member of the Muslim Joudeh family brings the key to the church to unlock and lock the door.

Have you ever experienced a time when you felt "born again again"? What happened?

What is the value in experiences like that?

EXPERIENTIAL DISCIPLESHIP

As the church transitioned from a grassroots movement to an institution in the late fourth century, the relational mode of discipleship gave way to a more experiential one. Buildings for worship were constructed, incense was burned, music was composed, and the Mass, or the re-creation of the passion narrative, was celebrated every week. In experiential discipleship, people were taught about Christ and grew in their relationship with Him through a full immersion into a medieval multimedia experience. Sights, sounds, and smells were strategically chosen to point people toward Christ.

List three words you tend to associate with medieval Christianity or the Catholic/Orthodox Church.

Is your view generally negative or positive? Why?

Experientialworship.com has many ideas and resources to lead you through experiential worship moments. For example, watch an interview with a potter as he throws a pot and describes each step—an experiential expression of the biblical metaphor of God the potter and His people the clay.

Listen to "Rock of Ages" by Chris Rice from the *Sacred Roads* playlist. Your group leader can e-mail you the whole playlist, or you can download it at *threadsmedia.com/sacredroads*.

Typically we think about this period of history as the Dark Ages, as a time of superstition, mystery, and in many cases, ignorance. It's true that during the medieval period of church history, or the time between Constantine and the Reformation, discipleship took on a very different form than many of us are comfortable with. But our discomfort doesn't mean there isn't validity to the way people in those days approached their relationships with Jesus.

ARCHITECTURE, ART, AND RITUAL

In the fourth century A.D., the church emerged from its hiding in the catacombs and living rooms and was thrust into the public square. Up until that time, the worst enemy of Christ-followers had been the Roman Emperor. Through persecution, violence, and pressure the empire had tried to stamp out this new fledgling religion. But then something world-shaking happened—Christianity won out. The emperor *became* a Christian and decided that Christianity was a good thing for his entire empire.

Following in the footsteps of Saul of Tarsus, another enemy of the faith, Constantine experienced a dramatic conversion that transitioned the emperor from the church's enemy to one of its most ardent champions. In A.D. 313, Constantine issued the Edict of Milan, which granted religious freedom to all forms of worship. The edict especially recognized the Christians and returned property that had been confiscated from them during the persecution of the early church. Christianity became the established religion of the empire.

What positive results can be associated with Constantine's Edict? What negative impacts might be associated with it?

The story goes that Constantine experienced a dramatic event in A.D. 312 at the Battle of Milvian Bridge that led to his conversion to Christianity. He looked up to the sun before the battle and saw a cross of light above it, and with it the Greek words meaning, "By this, conquer!" Constantine commanded his troops to adorn their shields with a Christian symbol, and they were victorious.

As a result of this newfound freedom, the church embraced the arts for the first time. Architecture, music, sculpture, and painting found a place in the life of the church, and the church utilized them as tools for teaching the illiterate. Constantine ordered church buildings built, and they were constructed at the perceived sacred sites in the Holy Land and throughout the Roman Empire.

The architecture of the church was strategic. The building itself was designed to direct people toward Christ and help them understand their relationship to Him. In *Church History in Plain Language*, Shelley explains that "the medieval church shot upward into the heavens, calling all below it to the glory of God."[12] Much of the architecture was reminiscent of the Old Testament tabernacle.

The basin of holy water, standing in the place of the tabernacle laver, reminded people of their need for cleansing. The primary room of the church, the nave, served as a kind of ark of the new covenant with the

Chartres Cathedral in France is an example of the Gothic style that developed in 12th-century Europe. Gothic architecture attempted to capture the essence of heaven through geometric design and the use of light.

high ceilings and ornate decoration speaking of the majesty of God. The layout, the symbols, and every single image meant something. The structure and its adornment pointed to the beauty and transcendence of God. In *Ancient-Future Faith*, Robert Webber explained, "Worship space was modeled after heaven."[13]

Have you ever thought about church architecture as a teaching tool?

Think about your own church. What sorts of things is the architecture teaching the people?

Along with architecture, various art forms were embraced as expressions of worship. In the first centuries of the church, art was not used in worship, and some even believed it to be a violation of the Second Commandment. But the fourth century marked a departure from this attitude, and the arts were harnessed as tools for teaching the fundamentals of faith to uneducated congregations. The Scriptures, inaccessible to most people because of their limited publication and the illiteracy of the people, were illustrated in paintings and sculpture. People were taught theology through a corporately understood visual language.

For instance, the color red typically symbolized "humanity" while the color blue was generally understood to represent "deity." In paintings of Jesus from this period, He is often depicted wearing a red robe over a blue tunic, symbolizing that Jesus was God who had taken on the form of man. People viewing these paintings learned basic theological truth about the divinity and humanity of Christ.

Have you ever been moved to worship by a piece of art? What was that experience like?

Take a virtual tour of the tabernacle and Solomon's temple, which replaced the tabernacle around 960 B.C., at *3dbibleproject.com*.

The movie screen is a type of modern-day stained glass, telling the stories of faith through pictures. Examples of such movies include *The Hiding Place; The Passion of the Christ; The Ten Commandments; Luther; The Lion, the Witch, and the Wardrobe; Chariots of Fire;* and *Amazing Grace.*

Ambrose was born into a Roman Christian family between about A.D. 337 and 340, the son of a soldier and a woman of intellect and piety. There is a legend that as an infant, a swarm of bees settled on his face while he lay in his cradle, leaving behind a drop of honey. His father considered this a sign of his future eloquence and honeyed tongue.

Curious how the Christian holidays you celebrate today compare to the festivals and feasts of the Old Testament? Consider the Threads study *Feast* for your next small group Bible study.

Hymns and poetry offered praise to God and also taught theology. Ambrose of Milan, typically considered the father of hymnology in the Latin Church, incorporated a form of singing into the life of faith that drew from the Greek symphonies and popular melodies of his day. Called the *Cantus Ambrosianus*, this mode of singing replaced the monotonous recitation of Psalms and prayers that had been the standard form of worship in the early church.

The home meetings of the early church were replaced by pageantry and celebration. Priests, adorned in colorful and ornately decorated clerical robes, led the people through a dramatic reflection on the sacrifice of Christ. This form of worship, called the Mass, became the centerpiece of corporate worship.

Webber describes the transition this way: "Because congregations were huge, it was necessary to shift worship from the intimacy of the first three centuries to theater. Drawing from the picture of worship in Revelation 4 and 5, earthly worship was patterned after heavenly worship. Consequently, considerable pomp and ceremony was introduced into worship: processions, great choirs, a more dramatic sermon style, fixed liturgies, vestments, sign of the cross, genuflection, and music forms such as the Gregorian Chant."[14]

The church calendar was also implemented. Festivals and feast days, reminiscent of the Old Testament Jewish festivals, were established. The calendar structured the entire year around the person, life, and work of Jesus Christ. Christmas and Easter were not simply days to be celebrated; they were seasons to be experienced. Thus, the daily lives of people were constantly saturated with and ordered by a religious rhythm.

The practice of the pilgrimage also came to prominence. Before Constantine's time, pilgrimage was not possible because of the oppression of the church. But when the emperor legalized Christianity, many people wanted to experience the story of Christ in the land where He lived. They wanted to touch the cross, visit the place of His birth, feel the waters of His Jordan River baptismal site, and see the rocky soil He described in the parable of the sower. They wanted to see what Jesus saw, touch what He felt, and hear what He heard.

Over time, the idea of pilgrimage took on the same mystical tone as the Mass. Pilgrims flocked to the Holy Land in search of a healing or forgiveness they believed was possible only in the sacred spaces of the holy sites.

Indeed, St. Jerome referred to the Holy Land as the "fifth Gospel," another revelation of the person of Jesus Christ. Theologians such as Gregory of Nyssa supported the value of pilgrimage while fighting against the notion that there was some sort of supernatural or mysterious quality or experience inherent in the Holy Land. Likewise, St. Jerome spoke highly of his own pilgrimage to Bethlehem, but warned of the dangers of falling too deeply into the notion that there was a mystical power in pilgrimage. Nevertheless, pilgrimage gave people the opportunity to experience the life and teachings of Christ in a very tangible way.

Which of these experiential practices appeal to you? Which do not? Why?

Can you think of any modern-day applications of them?

Many of these practices were abandoned by Protestants after the Reformation. In your estimation, was that a good idea or a bad idea? Why or why not?

Egeria's Travels, translated by John Wilkinson, is the best modern version of Egeria's pilgrimage diary.

"Jesus' whole life and preaching had only one aim: to reveal this inexhaustible, unlimited motherly and fatherly love of his God and to show the way to let that love guide every part of our daily lives. In his painting of the father, Rembrandt offers me a glimpse of that love. It is the love that always welcomes home and wants to celebrate."[15]
—Henri Nouwen

EXPERIENTIAL DISCIPLESHIP IN THE OLD TESTAMENT

In the Bible, the experiential approach to discipleship is probably first seen in the tabernacle, constructed during the wilderness wanderings of the Israelites. Serving as a symbol of God's presence in their midst, the tabernacle provided a process for encountering God in a real way.

While there are two chapters in the Bible dedicated to the creation of the world, there are 50 dedicated to the design, construction, and function of the tabernacle. God was very precise and gave instructions on even the smallest details of the tabernacle. In Exodus 31:1-5, God gave instructions on how this construction would be accomplished:

The word *tabernacle* means "tent of meeting." That's just what it was—not only the symbol of God's presence with His people, but also a structure demonstrating how a sinful man can come into the presence of a holy God.

To read more about the significance of the pieces of furniture in the tabernacle, check out *The Tabernacle: Shadows of the Messiah* by David Levy.

"The Lord also spoke to Moses: 'Look, I have appointed by name Bezalel son of Uri, son of Hur, of the tribe of Judah. I have filled him with God's Spirit, with wisdom, understanding, and ability in every craft to design artistic works in gold, silver, and bronze, to cut gemstones for mounting, and to carve wood for work in every craft.'"

How about that? The first person recorded in Scripture to be filled with the Holy Spirit was an artist responsible for the design and decoration of the tabernacle.

The tabernacle provided the people with a comprehensive and tangible way to connect with God. It was a multi-sensory engagement. Every piece of furniture, every action, and every smell was strategically designed and included by God in order to draw people closer to Him.

The brazen altar stood at the entrance and reminded the Israelites of their sin and need for sacrifice. The large bowl or laver, made with the mirrors of the women of Israel, reflected a person's image as they washed the sacrificial blood from their hands. The lampstand burned perpetually and illuminated the entire inner court, including the table of shewbread and the altar of incense. The most holy place contained the ark of the covenant and could only be entered once a year by the High Priest.

Entering the tabernacle must have been a sensory feast. Everything, everywhere, from the lighting to the wall hangings to the number of steps between each curtain, screamed theological truth. The tabernacle was an avenue for entering and experiencing the presence of God.

Scan through Exodus 25–31. What do you learn about God from His instructions for the construction of the tabernacle?

Should these instructions inform the design of our current spaces of worship? If so, how? If not, why not?

Now focus on Exodus 32. The formation of the golden calf was a perverted form of experiential worship. How can we tell the difference between God-honoring experiential worship and idolatrous experiential worship?

To find a museum in your area where you can spend some time with works of art, check out *museumspot.com*.

EXPERIENTIAL DISCIPLESHIP IN THE LIFE OF CHRIST

We often think of Jesus' discipleship methods as being highly relational. That is, He hung out with people and sort of just rubbed off on them. Jesus was definitely relational in His training of the Twelve, but He also gave them experiences. Whether telling a story or working a miracle, Jesus consistently invited people into experiences.

When Peter needed a lesson on God's provision, He set the stage for Peter to pull a coin from the mouth of a fish.

The story of Peter and the coin in the fish's mouth is recounted in Matthew 17:24-27, and Jesus washes the disciples' feet in John 13:1-17.

To teach His disciples about servanthood, He picked up the towel and let them feel the water wash over their feet.

The stories of Jesus were very tangible to the people who were hearing them. They touched real life and raw emotions. Healings and miracles put flesh on the principles being taught.

Imagine what the disciples must have thought as they passed around bottomless baskets of bread and fish to thousands of people. It was a discipleship experience they would never forget. No wonder the early church sold everything and gave to all as they had need—those original 12 disciples lived the theological truth that it is impossible to outgive God. They didn't learn that stewardship principle from an expository sermon; they learned it from real-life experiences.

What are some other experiences you wish you could have shared with Jesus?

Why do you think the experience is such a powerful tool for discipleship?

The ultimate experience occurred on the top of the mount of transfiguration. Peter, James, and John ascended the mountain with Jesus yet again for another long night of prayer. But Jesus had another discipleship experience prepared for them. Before their eyes, Jesus' appearance changed. Mark records that "His clothes became dazzling—extremely white as no launderer on earth could whiten them" (Mark 9:3). Moses and Elijah showed up to talk with Jesus.

And Jesus had invited Peter, James, and John to witness and participate. Jesus had already told them who He was. Now, He was letting them see, hear, and experience that truth.

The experience lasted for only a few moments. Then Jesus led them back down the mountain and into earthly life. But what kind of lasting impact did that moment have on those three men? How often did Peter, James, and John reflect on that time?

When John saw the glorified vision of Christ on the Isle of Patmos in Revelation 1, did his memory race back to the mount of transfiguration? Was the vision of Christ similar to the one he saw so many years ago?

The experience certainly impacted Peter, as we can see from his reflections later in the New Testament:

"For we did not follow cleverly contrived myths when we made known to you the power and coming of our Lord Jesus Christ; instead, we were eyewitnesses of His majesty. For when He received honor and glory from God the Father, a voice came to Him from the Majestic Glory: 'This is My beloved Son. I take delight in Him!' And we heard this voice when it came from heaven while we were with Him on the holy mountain. So we have the prophetic word strongly confirmed. You will do well to pay attention to it, as to a lamp shining in a dismal place, until the day dawns and the morning star arises in your hearts" (2 Peter 1:16-19).

It was truly a mountain-top experience for them. As Peter said in Mark 9:5, "Rabbi, it is good for us to be here!" The transfiguration gave Peter encouragement, confidence, and hope throughout his life.

> **Read Mark 9:2-13. What did Jesus teach or reveal to His disciples through this experience?**

Jesus talked with Moses and Elijah during the transfiguration, but what did they talk about? Luke 9:31 literally says they discussed Jesus' "departure." That word can also be translated as "exodus." Jesus, Moses, and Elijah all experienced an exodus. Moses led the people out of Egypt, Elijah was taken from the world in a blazing chariot, and Jesus would lead people into freedom from the bondage of sin.

Describe a time when you experienced Jesus in a new way.

EXPERIENTIAL DISCIPLESHIP IN THE NEW TESTAMENT

The experiential approach played a prominent role in the discipleship of the early church. In Acts 2, we read that the early followers of Christ were in awe of the miracles and signs of the Holy Spirit around them. Sermons were not simply spoken; they were experienced.

Some practices of the early church were actually forms of experiential discipleship. The initiation for new Christians was the symbolically rich rite of baptism. This outward expression of an inward reality demonstrated in a very tangible way the death and burial of a person's old life and his or her resurrection into a new life in Christ. The person baptized experienced a physical and dramatic re-enactment of spiritual rebirth. Those early baptisms occurred outside in public, thereby allowing the baptismal candidates to share their stories. In this way, baptism became experiential not only for the people being submerged, but also for everyone in attendance.

Likewise, Communion, or the Lord's Supper, invited believers into a re-enactment of the story of redemption. Communion was not simply an afterthought or an activity tagged on quarterly to a worship service. Rather, the practice of remembering the body and blood of Christ was the centerpiece of the gathering of believers. Communion is a virtual pilgrimage across space and time to the foot of the cross in order to remember and meditate on what Christ did for us there.

You'll find an account of the first Lord's Supper in Matt. 26:17-30. Jesus established this practice with His disciples while observing Passover before His crucifixion.[16]

How are baptism and communion discipleship experiences?

What are some things you can intentionally do to make communion a more significant opportunity for spiritual growth in your life?

Nikolaus Ludwig von Zinzendorf was a German religious and social reformer and bishop of the Moravian Church. Along with his theological contributions, Zinzendorf was an avid sender of missionaries to places like the West Indies and Greenland.

PUTTING IT INTO PRACTICE

The experiential form of discipleship is still emphasized today by the Catholic, Anglican, and Orthodox traditions, and it's reflected in their architecture, incense, music, iconography, and art. However, people from all denominational persuasions throughout history have been drawn to Christ through experiential forms of discipleship.

Count Zinzendorf, founder of the Moravian movement, traced his faith journey back to an image of Christ crucified that had a profound impact on him. Henri Nouwen's call to minister to the mentally disabled was confirmed by his meditation on Rembrandt's *The Return of the Prodigal Son*. Mark Batterson, a 21st-century pastor in Washington, D.C., originally came to Christ after seeing a story of faith in the film, *The Hiding Place*. Despite its flaws when taken too far, the experiential form of discipleship in its purest form is a very valuable tool to help people step into the story of their faith.

Experiential discipleship moves our faith well beyond listening to a lecture or sitting in the sanctuary pews for an hour. In experiential discipleship, our faith becomes fully integrated into the fabric of our lives. We find both reality and mystery.

> **Write down three experiences that taught you something about Jesus or otherwise helped you grow in your faith. What did you learn from each?**

To locate a retreat center in your area available for a weekend of spiritual reflection, visit *findthedivine.com*.

RETREATS

One of the most common expressions of experiential discipleship today is the spiritual formation retreat. Almost every denomination facilitates retreat experiences for their congregations. Some encourage retreats that create space for silence, solitude, and meditation, while other retreats are designed to help people connect to others with similar interests. Regardless of the purpose, they revolve around experiential discipleship. The retreat is such an effective means for experience because of the focused intensity of a few short days or even hours.

Batterson, my lead pastor at National Community Church (NCC), developed a simple formula: Change of Pace + Change of Place = Change in Perspective.

Retreats offer us a change of pace. We need to slow down and find time to recharge our spiritual batteries and recalibrate our lives according to Scripture. Jesus did this. He only had three years to finish His ministry, but He spent the first 40 days of the ministry fasting in the wilderness.

Retreats also offer a change of place. Exodus 33:7 says:

"Now Moses took a tent and set it up outside the camp, far away from the camp; he called it the tent of meeting. Anyone who wanted to consult the Lord would go to the tent of meeting that was outside the camp."

Moses went outside the camp to commune with God. He needed a change of place, so he moved outside the realm of his ministry to connect with God. The result is a change in perspective. Sometimes you just need to move out of the ordinary to have an extraordinary encounter with God. Here are some practical ideas to make it happen:

- If your church offers a retreat, go on it.
- Take a retreat from your daily routine a few times during the week. Spend time in prayer and reflection.
- Find a relaxing location where you can get away from the nine-to-five world for a few days. Go alone and soke up the silence.
- Gather a few friends and plan your own retreat. Go on a hike. Go to a sacred space. Crash at a friend's house. Just go someplace that allows you to change your pace, place, and perspective.

As a way to try out experiential discipleship, watch the video called "Communion" during your small group discussion. This video will help you see and then take the Lord's Supper with a new and fresh perspective. You can also download the video for yourself at *threadsmedia.com/sacredroads.*

Some might argue that retreats are merely mountain-top experiences and not true life-changing discipleship. While I would agree that retreats, without a daily encounter with Christ, result in nothing more than a shallow spiritual high, a retreat can jumpstart us spiritually, provide an opportunity to reconnect with God and others, or give us a completely new perspective. I can't imagine that Peter, James, and John remembered the mount of transfiguration as nothing more than a spiritual high and an unimportant step in their training. Why else would Jesus have taken His closest three followers on that journey?

What is one change of place and pace that has given you a change in perspective?

What makes a change of place and pace a spiritual experience?

A pilgrimage, in its simplest form, is a journey to a place of significance. The movie *Elizabethtown* is about such a pilgrimage. Take a look at this 2005 film.

To read more about one young adult's experience with pilgrimage, check out *Sacred Travels* by Christian George.

PILGRIMAGE

Another form of experiential discipleship is pilgrimage. Contrary to popular opinion, pilgrimage is not a lost discipline in our Western culture; it just takes on different forms. Baseball fans flock to stadium after stadium on a quest to visit every shrine of their favorite national pastime. Similarly, hundreds of people descend upon Graceland every year to visit the grave of a man who changed history by swinging his hips on television.

No, pilgrimage isn't a lost practice. But as a tool for spiritual formation, it has faded into the background of our faith history, viewed as an outdated activity of odd desert monks, thrill-seeking explorers, or misguided crusaders.

My own journey to the Holy Land led me to a new conclusion: Pilgrimage should be resurrected and promoted as an important tool for spiritual formation. The call of pilgrimage connects with the inner cravings deep inside us, where we know intuitively that the Christian life is a greater journey than a 100-foot walk down the center aisle of a church. Faith is a lifelong journey, and pilgrimage appeals to our yearnings to enter into outward physical expressions of our inward faith journeys. It gives us a sense of history, context, and authenticity.

But there's a big difference between being tourists and being pilgrims. Tourists take pictures to share with friends and family after returning home. Pilgrims take pictures for the same reason that the patriarchs built altars—to commemorate the work of God in their lives. Tourists are interested in their schedules. Pilgrims are interested in their transformation. Tourists pass through the land. Pilgrims allow the land to pass through them.

As St. Jerome or St. Gregory of Nyssa would argue, there is nothing particularly sacred about places. The Church of the Holy Sepulcher doesn't contain some inherent mystical quality. God can reveal Himself to His people in any place and any time. But there was something about the Holy Land that helped me understand and connect with God in a way that was different than ever before.

But you don't have to travel the world—pilgrimage can also be found closer to home. It can be any journey that puts feet to your faith and connects you to God's story. Here are some ideas for pilgrimages that might be a little more accessible than Jerusalem:

- Go to a historic church to meditate and pray.
- Spend a day at an art museum containing paintings that depict the life of Christ.
- Return to the place of your salvation or baptism.
- Return to a place where a significant event in your spiritual journey took place.
- Watch a travel documentary about the Holy Land.

List some places of spiritual significance in your life that could be pilgrimage destinations.

Do you think we can hear God speak more clearly to us in certain holy or sacred places? What scriptural basis supports your answer?

In A.D. 326, Constantine's 79-year-old mother Helena made a famous pilgrimage to Jerusalem. On this trip, she was baptized in the Jordan River and, as legend has it, discovered the cross of Christ. It was at this site that she had her son erect the Church of the Holy Sepulcher. Helena went on to remove pagan worship sites and build churches at places of significance in Christian history.

STATIONS OF THE CROSS

While pilgrimage allows us to have real experiences in the actual places of history, the Stations of the Cross were designed to give us the opportunity to go on a virtual pilgrimage.

The Stations of the Cross is an experiential devotional tool that allows us to enter into the story of the passion of Christ through what Richard Foster would call "the sanctified imagination."

For centuries, Christians have journeyed to the Holy Land to walk in the actual footsteps of Jesus. They follow a path known as the *Via Dolorosa* (literally, "Way of Sorrow"), which is believed to be the actual route Jesus moved along from Pilate's court to His crucifixion at Golgotha to His burial in the tomb.

Many of the traditional Stations of the Cross would be familiar to you. For example, station 1 is when Jesus is condemned to death. Station 11 is the crucifixion, and station 12 is the death of Jesus. But there are also stations that you might be less familiar with, like station 6 when Jesus' face is wiped or station 8 when Jesus meets the daughters of Jerusalem.

The early literature does not specify a number of stations. They range from 7 to 37. By the 17th century, 14 stations seemed to be the most common number and the Roman Catholic Church formalized it. The 14 Stations of the Cross trace Jesus' path from Pilate's house to Golgotha to His tomb, mixing some events we find in Scripture with some that come to us via the tradition of the church.

Thousands of pilgrims still trek to the Holy Land every year to walk the Stations of the Cross in Jerusalem. But Catholic churches have erected symbolic representations of each of the 14 stations in their sanctuaries to allow congregants to go on a virtual pilgrimage. The stations have been depicted through drawing, painting, sculpture, stained glass, and wood-carving. Recently, the stations have even appeared on the Internet. Led by a priest or minister, the congregation proceeds from station to station, pausing at each for relevant Scripture reading, prayer, meditation, and singing.

One of the greatest dangers we face spiritually is remembering what we should forget and forgetting what we should remember. People in the Bible were always making altars to remember what God had done for them. The Stations of the Cross are altars where we can stop and remember. It's an opportunity to connect with Christ in a very raw way.

Here are some ideas for implementing this ancient experiential devotional practice into your own spiritual formation activities:

- Watch *The Passion of the Christ*. Stop the movie occasionally to meditate on the Scriptural references along the way.
- Meditate on the Passion narratives in the four Gospels, and identify your own "stations"—the moments in the narrative that speak most to you. Write out a devotional thought or prayer for each station.

What benefits do you see in Stations of the Cross? What negatives do you see?

What are some other forms of experiential discipleship?

Since pilgrimage to the Holy Land required a tremendous financial investment, replicas of the *Via Dolorosa* were soon erected throughout Europe so that people could participate in the devotional exercise without going to Jerusalem.

If you have watched Mel Gibson's *The Passion of the Christ,* then you have also experienced the Stations of the Cross. He used the traditional 14 stations as the storyboard for the movie.

DARE TO EXPLORE

If you come from an evangelical tradition like me, some of these practices may seem foreign, mystical, and even uncomfortable. But the first 12 disciples of Jesus would likely find our traditional classroom models of discipleship equally foreign. Jesus offered spiritual growth experiences "along the way." Most of His teaching moments were pulled from the day-to-day experiences of life—at parties, on fishing expeditions, on road trips, while paying taxes, and while preparing lunch. Some of the most significant lessons the disciples learned occurred during storms, meals, funerals, and weddings.

Jesus instructs us to love Him with all our heart, soul, mind, and strength. That means that 50 percent of the love due Him comes from our emotions and passions. It's OK to experience Him and grow from that experience. Dare to step out and try something new. Dare to explore an ancient spiritual discipline to unlock new opportunities for spiritual growth. And continue to appreciate the forms of experiential discipleship we are more familiar with—baptism and communion.

But while you're exploring, beware of the pitfalls and potential problems that are often associated with this form of discipleship. Without grounding in the Scripture, odd theologies and methodologies can develop. It's easy for experiential discipleship to dissolve into religion that becomes a performance, always looking toward the fantastical. If you aren't careful, your spiritual growth will begin to ride the highs and lows of subjective experiences as opposed to being based on the foundational and timeless truths of the Word of God. That's why it's important to be in relationship with others who can bring wisdom and warning. It's critical to be grounded in the Word of God to ensure that your experience falls in line with the truth of Scripture. And it's imperative that the experience fuel your desire and ability to reach out to others.

It's also important that we remember that worship is about God . . . not about us. It's ultimately about creating an experience around the throne of God (Revelation 4) and not about consistently seeking an experience of our own.

> **What pitfalls or problems can you identify that could be related to the relational form of discipleship?**

Listen to the audio segment called "Experimenting with Experiential Discipleship" this week. Your group leader will send it to you via e-mail, or you can download it at *threadsmedia. com/sacredroads*. These audio recordings are designed to help you connect with different expressions of discipleship.

ANOTHER VOICE—ANOTHER ERA
JOHANN SEBASTIAN BACH (1685–1750)

Johann Sebastian Bach composed some of the most technically and spiritually important pieces of the Baroque period. A devout Christian, Bach desired to create music that enhanced the preaching of the Word. He said, "Music's only purpose should be the glory of God and the recreation of the human spirit."[17]

Trained on the organ and violin, he became the cantor at St. Thomas's School in Leipzig, Germany, and he served as the organist and music director for two Lutheran churches. During his first six years in Leipzig, Bach wrote up to five annual cantata cycles, many expounding on the Gospel readings for the Sunday worship in the Lutheran church. His composition style seemed to match the style of preaching in the Lutheran tradition.

Dr. Paul Minear of Yale Divinity School said, "He had a life-time calling from God to create forms of music appropriate to God's praise. His love for the Bible and the church was translated into a passion to fuse faith and music, theology and liturgy, perhaps we should say, to choreograph 'the dance of God.' He set to music the biblical story in such a way as to reveal God's presence to the congregation and to elicit an intimate, though often also disturbing, conversation with the Almighty."[18] Bach produced more than 1,000 works, including *The Passion of St. John*, *Christmas Oratorio*, and *Mass in B Minor*.

TRY IT OUT

Memorize Psalm 34:8: *"Taste and see that the LORD is good; blessed is the man who takes refuge in Him."*

The Louvre Museum in France is home to some of history's greatest works of art, many of which are biblically themed. Visit *louvre.fr* and you can take a virtual tour this week. Take the tour with journal in hand, and write out your thoughts as you practice this form of experiential discipleship.

NOTES

session three
Intellectual Discipleship

Lingering at the podium as his students filed out of the lecture room, Philipp breathed a quick prayer for his students, "God, help them learn the language so they might love You better." He was pleased with the holy curiosity and questions of his students and truly loved his new job, despite the cold reception he had received a few weeks prior. Philipp was only 20 years old, but the university's founder had granted him a position, leading some on the faculty to question whether he was experienced and mature enough for his post.

Which reminded him—he was late for a meeting. He packed his books and sped hurriedly to the office of the celebrated but unpredictable and eccentric monk, scholar, and professor. Philipp was looking forward to the meeting. More than a year ago, the professor had published a statement that was still causing serious waves and concerns for church leadership. That was the kind of person Philipp wanted to learn from. He was a thinker—so was Philipp. As thinkers, they agreed that the more people could learn about God, the more they could love Him and live according to His perfect plan. How could they worship Him if they didn't even know what they were worshiping? Go back to the source—the original text, the language of the writers—and discover the truth. That was Philipp's goal, and the professor shared his sentiment.

As Philipp entered his office, the professor offered him a chair and showed him the manuscript he was working on. It was a letter to the university's founder, Prince Frederick, that read, "We soon recovered from the prejudices excited by his stature and appearance; we now praise and admire his eloquence."

"Thank you, Professor." Philipp meant it with much more emotion than his words revealed. And that was the end of their obligatory social exchanges. They opened up the Greek New Testament and began to worship—a form of worship they experienced together as they discovered truths, meanings, and insight from the Scripture.

Philipp Melanchthon was a key player in the Protestant Reformation and (eventually) a good friend of the "eccentric" professor Martin Luther.

ARGUMENTS

There were debates all the time:

Baptism: *Should we sprinkle or immerse?*
The Holy Spirit: *Do the spiritual gifts still operate today? In what ways?*
The nature of the church, clergy, and preaching: *Which ecclesiological perspective is correct?*

I met Quinn during my sophomore year of engineering studies at Louisiana State University, and our friendship began when he lopped a friendly arm around my shoulder in Dr. Bengtson's office as we set our schedules for the upcoming semester. For the next three years, we spent valuable time together—studying, breaking dorm rules, and playing ridiculous amounts of Nintendo. And often, the conversation turned to God. We were both studying environmental engineering, but we were both deeply committed to our relationships with Christ and our roles in the church. We were also fiercely loyal to our respective theological foundations, and that led to many passionate diatribes.

The more we argued, the more I learned. And every time I learned, two things happened: I became more certain what I believed and why I believed it, and I grew in my respect of those who belonged to a different branch of the body of Christ. Our relationship was an example of iron sharpening iron, and I developed a broader understanding of many doctrines I thought I understood well.

Do arguments cause you to grow in your faith or falter in your faith?

Studylight.org is a user-friendly site with free commentaries, word studies, and Greek and Hebrew resources to aid you in your examination of the Bible.

A Beautiful Mind won the Academy Award for best picture in 2002. It tells the story of intellectual professor John Nash and his battle with his own mind. It's interesting to watch while digesting the intellectual approach to discipleship.

INTELLECTUAL DISCIPLESHIP

As the Dark Ages lifted, the world became more driven by science than superstition, and more by reason than religion. The Renaissance, the Age of Reason, and the Age of Enlightenment elevated the importance and primacy of logic over experience. New voices emerged in the theological debate and introduced an intellectual approach to discipleship. In intellectual discipleship, people were taught about Christ and grew in their relationship with Him through a systematic, academic study of Scripture and the writings of godly teachers.

In what ways are reason and religion compatible? In what ways are they incompatible?

Are the words "academic" and "growing in Christ" related in your mind? Why or why not?

Pastor and author Mark Buchanan said, "Any deep change in how we live begins with a deep change in how we think."[19] That's what happened in the period following the Dark Ages. The Protestant Reformation coincided roughly with the Age of Enlightenment. The movement was fueled by modern technology—the invention of the printing press—and the doctrine of *Sola Scriptura*—the belief that Scripture is the only inerrant and infallible authority for Christian faith.

New philosophies and new forms of thinking, based on logic and reason, influenced the way Scripture was read and applied. The emphasis on experience was diminished as new theological understandings led to the formation of new congregations and denominations. It's from this period of history that we see the introduction of inductive Bible study, systematic theology, apologetics, and the writings of the church fathers.

Consider Mark Buchanan's claim that "any deep change in how we live begins with a deep change in how we think." Do you agree or disagree? Why?

Inductive Bible study is the process of allowing the Scriptures to speak for themselves by following the three-step process of observation, interpretation, and application.

Deductive Bible study is the search for passages to support conclusions we have already reached.

Exegesis is the careful, systematic study of Scripture to determine the original, intended meaning, while hermeneutics seeks to properly interpret the text so that we understand what it means for us today.

A BROKEN SYSTEM

In 1095, Pope Urban II called on Christians to go on crusade to regain the Holy Land. *Deus Volt*—"God wills it"—became the battle cry against the Muslims who had taken possession of Jerusalem. Over the next 200 years, thousands answered the call. They went seeking fame, fortune, and forgiveness. It was experiential discipleship gone bad, a perverted form of pilgrimage.

The sale of indulgences was one of the key church practices Martin Luther spoke out against in his 95 Theses that launched the Protestant Reformation. Thesis 45 states, "Christians are to be taught that he who sees a man in need, and passes him by, and gives [his money] for pardons, purchases not the indulgences of the pope, but the indignation of God" (*theopedia.com/95_Theses*).

In May 1518, Tetzel responded to Luther's 95 Theses with his own 50 theses, which skipped over the sale of indulgences and focused on the authority of the church.

Then, at the Council of Clermont, Pope Urban II took the Crusade to the next level, declaring that participation in the so-called "holy war" was the equivalent of complete penance. That is to say that if you participated in the holy war, all of your sins would be absolutely forgiven. That decree brought the idea of "indulgence"—or the selling of salvation—into full practice. The indulgence system took off and expanded beyond the Crusade. For the next 400 years, the sale of indulgences by "professional pardoners" escalated to appalling proportions.

In 1392, the indulgence system was so rampant that Pope Boniface IX was forced to condemn it. The scandal rose to a breaking point in 1517 when Pope Leo X authorized an indulgence for contributions toward the building of St. Peter's Basilica in Rome. When salesman extraordinaire John Tetzel was unleashed with his now infamous pitch, "As soon as a coin in the coffer rings, a soul from purgatory springs," an idealistic and passionate monk picked a fight that led to one of the most significant turning points in church history—the Protestant Reformation.

Can you think of any modern-day equivalents of the sale of indulgences?

Why is such a system so offensive?

On October 31, 1517, Martin Luther posted the 95 Theses on the door of the Castle Church in Wittenberg, Germany, and called for a debate on many questionable practices of the Catholic Church. But in his harsh criticism, Luther never wanted to split from the church; he wanted to reform it. Between 1517 and 1520, Luther was called before a series of hearings and debates. In 1520, the pope excommunicated him. In 1521, the Holy Roman Emperor Charles V summoned Luther to appear at the Diet of Worms, where he was ordered to recant—take back his criticisms and beliefs. Luther's response summed up the emerging theology of the time:

"Unless I am convinced by the testimony of Scripture or by clear reason, for I do not trust in the pope or in councils alone, since it is well known that they have erred and contradicted themselves, I am bound by the Scriptures that I have quoted and my conscience is captive to the Word of God. I cannot and I will not retract anything; for it is neither safe nor right to go against conscience. I cannot do otherwise; here I stand, may God help me. Amen."[20]

Which part of Luther's response resonates the strongest with you?

What beliefs would you be willing to die for?

The pomp and circumstance of the church had become such a spectator sport that Luther and his Reformer buddies were compelled to leave behind the touchy-feely experiential stuff and concentrate simply on the text of the Bible and the importance of the renewal of the mind. In the Reformation, the pulpit replaced the altar as the centerpiece of the worship experience. The pageantry of the multi-sensory celebration of the Mass was replaced with the logical and plainly communicated teaching from Scripture. As Shelley explains, "The whole emphasis in worship changed from the celebration of the sacrificial Mass to the preaching and teaching of God's Word."[21]

What do you think should be in the center of the worship experience—the altar or the pulpit? Why?

What Scripture supports your answer?

The Reformation flowed in two streams. Martin Luther led the effort in Germany while John Calvin pioneered the Reformed movement in Switzerland. Luther's central doctrine was justification by faith while Calvin's focused on the sovereignty of God.

Also known as "All Saints Church," the Castle Church in Wittenberg has been acknowledged as the most famous building in Wittenberg. Martin Luther and Philipp Melanchthon, a friend of Luther's and fellow reformer, are both buried in the church. Luther's tomb is located below the pulpit.

The theological framework of the Protestant Reformation can be summarized by the five *sola* (meaning "one" or "only") statements. *Sola Scriptura* (by Scripture alone), *sola fide* (by faith alone), *sola gratia* (by grace alone), *solus Christus* (by Christ alone) and *soli Deo gloria* (glory to God alone).

The Reformer John Calvin was 12 years old when Luther was excommunicated. His views of salvation, Scripture, and the church were similar to those of Luther, and he placed a high value on the importance of learning, insisting that clergy be intellectuals. He taught that preachers must know Scripture, understand doctrine, demonstrate godliness of character, and possess the gift of teaching. He also insisted that they be conscientious students.

The Age of Reason was seeded by the Reformation and Renaissance, and came into full bloom in the mid 1600s. New philosophies and new forms of thinking, based on logic and reason, influenced the way Scripture was read and applied. As Shelley explained, "The Age of Reason was nothing less than an intellectual revolution, a whole new way of looking at God, the world, and one's self."[22]

While this movement posed new threats and challenges to the Christian faith, it also offered new opportunities. Modern science emerged and men like Blaise Pascal embraced the mystery of faith while using logic to explain it. Scholars began to place the Bible under the microscope of reason to discover the truth of God for themselves.

Where do you see faith along the spectrum of mystery and logic? Is it more mysterious? Or is it more reasonable?

What can each approach learn from the other?

But let's look even further back, because loving God with the mind didn't start during the High Middle Ages. We see the dawning of intellectual approaches to God thousands of years earlier.

INTELLECTUAL DISCIPLESHIP IN THE OLD TESTAMENT

After a tumultuous end to his father David's reign, Solomon ascended to the throne of Israel in 970 B.C. He is associated most with wealth, women, writing, and wisdom. He wrote three books: Song of Solomon was written early in his life to celebrate the joys of marriage; Proverbs contains nuggets of wisdom for daily living; and Ecclesiastes records the futile search for meaning in life outside a relationship with God.

You may have used one of Pascal's methods of reasoning before, but hopefully not in regards to God's existence. Being unable to prove the existence of God through reason, Pascal decided that you are better to wager as though God exists, because you have everything to gain if He does and nothing to lose if He doesn't. Compared with the other option—that you wager God doesn't exist only to find out He does—the former seemed like a much better option to Pascal. This is known as Pascal's Wager.

In 1 Kings 3, God appeared to Solomon and asked him the simple question, "What should I give you?" Solomon asked for "an obedient heart to judge" and the ability to "discern between good and evil" (1 Kings 3:5,9). God was so impressed with Solomon's request that He granted it, and granted it in a big way. We see evidence of God's gift throughout Solomon's story. Apparently, Solomon's wisdom wasn't confined to religious knowledge; rather, God gifted him with the desire and capacity to grow in his knowledge of the world around him. In 1 Kings 4:33-34, we read:

He described trees, from the cedar in Lebanon to the hyssop growing out of the wall. He also taught about animals, birds, reptiles, and fish. People came from everywhere, [sent] by every king on earth who had heard of his wisdom, to listen to Solomon's wisdom.

We also see evidence of Solomon's desire for others to pursue wisdom and encouragement in his writings:

A wise man will listen and increase his learning, and a discerning man will obtain guidance—for understanding a proverb or a parable, the words of the wise, and their riddles. The fear of the Lord is the beginning of knowledge; fools despise wisdom and instruction (Proverbs 1:5-7).

Solomon often equates wisdom and knowledge with the fear of the Lord. What do you think it means to fear the Lord?

How is the fear of God related to wisdom?

Scripture says that Solomon's annual income was 25 tons of gold, and that did not include trade (1 Kings 10:14). He placed heavy taxes on Israel to fund his extravagant living, which included drinking cups that were solid gold. Scripture tells us that the Queen of Sheba was breathless when she saw Solomon's riches (1 Kings 10:4-5).

Eventually, Solomon's desire for wealth and women overpowered the wisdom God gave him, and his life spiraled downward into a meaningless existence. The Book of Ecclesiastes, written toward the end of his life as a sort of memoir, reveals a man at the end of his rope. Despite Solomon's fame, fortune, and success, Ecclesiastes was written in some of the most dismal and despairing tones in the Bible. The book nevertheless contains some of the most compelling exhortations to honor God in the way you live and think.

What does Solomon's story and writing reveal about intellectual discipleship?

The kingdom of Judah was ruled by both good kings who encouraged the nation to worship God and by evil kings who imported pagan religious practices. Some of the good kings included Asa (1 Kings 15:9-24; 2 Chronicles 14–16), Jehoshaphat (1 Kings 22:41-50; 2 Chronicles 17–21:3), Uzziah (2 Kings 15:1-7; 2 Chronicles 26), and Hezekiah (2 Kings 18–20). Josiah was the last of the good kings.

Another example of how educating the mind leads to changed lives can be found in the story of King Josiah (2 Kings 22–23). Josiah, who was crowned at the ripe old age of eight, inherited a corrupt political and religious system from his father Amon and grandfather Manasseh. Eighteen years into Josiah's reign, the priests discovered the "book of the Law" in the temple. Many scholars believe this to be the Book of Deuteronomy. After reading it and consulting spiritual authority, Josiah tore his clothes and personally repented. Then, he had all the people assemble to hear the reading of the Law and implemented widespread religious reforms. The nation of Israel experienced revival when they discovered, read, and applied the Word of God.

What lessons can we learn from the life of Josiah to ensure that we actually apply the Word of God and don't just learn about it?

INTELLECTUAL DISCIPLESHIP IN THE LIFE OF CHRIST

Dallas Willard refers to Jesus as the "most intelligent man that ever lived."[23] We catch a glimpse of His intelligence early in His life when His parents discovered Him in the temple discussing spiritual questions with religious leaders. Scripture tells us in Luke 2:47 that these well-educated teachers were "astounded at His understanding and His answers."

A quick survey of the Book of Matthew reveals several instances where Jesus engaged in intellectual discipleship:

- He relied on His mental grasp of Scripture during the temptation in the wilderness, recalling Old Testament writings He had committed to memory in order to defeat Satan's advances (Matthew 4:1-11).

- He revealed the weaknesses in the philosophy of the Pharisees by identifying their logical inconsistencies. For example, consider His clash with the Pharisees in Matthew 12:1-14 concerning what work was and was not permissible on the Sabbath.

- He entered into a theological debate with the Gentile woman in Matthew 15:21-28 before healing her daughter.

- He followed the model of the great rabbis by teaching through questions. Whenever Jesus' enemies tried to trap Him in a tough question, He would respond with a question that turned the conversation upside down (Matthew 21:23-27; 22:15-22).

In each of these instances and many others, Jesus used logic, teaching, and intellectual discipleship to reveal a picture of faith to others and to spur His listeners to a deeper understanding and greater desire for spiritual growth.

> **How do you react to Willard's statement that Jesus was the most intelligent man who has ever lived?**

> **Do you typically think of Jesus as intelligent? Why or why not?**

INTELLECTUAL DISCIPLESHIP IN THE NEW TESTAMENT

In Acts 17, Paul boldly marched into the Areopagus, the center of Greek philosophical debate, and threw down with the best minds in Athens. He used their philosophy, their religion, and their artistic influences to reveal that Jesus Christ was the unknown God they had been worshiping for years in order to convince them to follow Him as the one true God. The showdown was a mix of oratorical skill, cultural exegesis, and philosophical proof empowered by the Holy Spirit.

In that attempt, Paul seemed to be very literally living out the Great Commission. Jesus' last command to His followers was that they go everywhere and make disciples. The word "disciple" comes from the Greek word *mathetes*, which means "learner." The Greek word for repentance, *metanoia*, literally means "a change of mind."

Listen to the audio segment called "Experimenting with Intellectual Discipleship" this week. Your group leader will send it to you via e-mail, or you can download it at *threadsmedia.com/sacredroads*. These audio recordings are designed to help you connect with different expressions of discipleship.

The Areopagus on Mars' Hill is located northwest of the Acropolis in Athens. Greek mythology says it's where the god Ares was put on trial when Poseidon accused him of murdering his son, Halirrhotius.

In fact, much of the New Testament was written to correct wrong ideas that had crept into the church. Peter, Paul, John, and others warned their readers to be vigilant, stand against wrong beliefs, and actively seek the truth. First Peter 1:13 sums it up nicely: "Get your minds ready for action." If we are going to grow into the people God has created us to be, we must sharpen our minds, allow our intellects to be transformed by God, and prepare them for action.

Changing our minds does a lot more than make us think more deeply. The writings of Paul include strong exhortations to change our behaviors by changing our minds. Paul instructed his readers to "be transformed by the renewing of your mind" (Romans 12:2). Ephesians 4:20-24 explains sanctification and includes the process, "You are being renewed in the spirit of your minds." The church at Corinth was encouraged to develop the mind of Christ (1 Corinthians 2:16). Galatians and Romans are the most intellectually stimulating and theologically dense books in the Bible. Romans in particular sparked three of the most significant developments in theological and ecclesiological history: Augustine and the concept of original sin, Luther and the concept of justification by faith, and Calvin and the concept of the sovereignty of God.

Paul ardently challenged his disciple, the young pastor Timothy, to give himself to the study of Scripture. Consider his advice in the second letter he wrote:

"All Scripture is inspired by God and is profitable for teaching, for rebuking, for correcting, for training in righteousness, so that the man of God may be complete, equipped for every good work" (2 Timothy 3:16-17).

> **How has the study of Scripture prepared you for good works? Describe a time when you saw one of the four purposes of Scripture at work in your own life (teaching, rebuking, correction, or training).**

The list could go on and on. The end result is a conclusion that we are called to love God with our minds. We are to study, internalize, dwell on, memorize, and apply the Word of God. In Acts 17, we are introduced to a group of people called the Bereans. Luke commended them because they didn't just listen to his instruction but studied the Bible for themselves to ascertain the veracity of his teachings:

R

Long before the Reformation, in the 12th century, a new movement emerged called Scholasticism. The Scholastics sought to explain the accepted doctrines of the church through faith, reason, Scripture, and tradition. They insisted that the faith they embraced was not blind but "faith invested by grace with reason and imagination."

They pursued two goals: 1) to reconcile Christian doctrine and belief with human reason, and 2) to systematically arrange the teachings of the church into an orderly theological system. Thomas Aquinas, the most famous of the Scholastics, published his system in *Summa Theologica*.

"The people here were more open-minded than those in Thessalonica, since they welcomed the message with eagerness and examined the Scriptures daily to see if these things were so" (Acts 17:11).

APPLICATIONS

A. W. Tozer said, "A right conception of God is basic not only to systematic theology but to practical Christian living as well . . . there is scarcely an error in doctrine or a failure in applying Christian ethics that cannot be traced finally to imperfect and ignoble thoughts about God."[24] Let's consider three ways we can grow in our knowledge for the purpose of being transformed into Christ-likeness.

BIBLE STUDY

Bible study may sound like a stale, academic process. But when we read the Bible correctly, its stories and teachings spring to life. Before we launch into how to read and study the Word of God, let's consider why it's even important.

Why Study the Bible?

First, and perhaps most obvious, we should study the Bible because it teaches us about God. Psalm 119:12 declares, "LORD, may You be praised; teach me Your statutes." There's a connection between worship and knowing the Word of God. The more you know of God, the more you love God, and the more you're thankful for who He is and what He has done for you.

Secondly, it teaches us how to live. Psalm 119:11 says, "I have treasured Your word in my heart so that I may not sin against You." From improving our marriages to managing our finances to making simple decisions, the Bible gives us principles for how to live.

Finally, the Bible gives us purpose and a sense of destiny. Most of us tend to view this book as a set of religious or moral principles that must be embraced or obeyed. Some view it as a systematic theology. It's been used by people as a science textbook, an anthropology manual, and a political platform. Though the Bible certainly speaks to all of those things, none of them define its primary purpose—to tell God's story. It begins with God and ends with God, and our lives are found somewhere in the middle. And it's when we understand God's story and see our lives against that backdrop that we begin to discover answers to those age-old questions: Who am I? Why am I here? What is my purpose in life?

Watch the motion picture *Luther* (2003) for a cinematic telling of the life and times of Martin Luther, one of the key players in the development of intellectual discipleship.

Listen to "Come Thou Fount of Every Blessing" by Sufjan Stevens from the *Sacred Roads* playlist. Your group leader can e-mail you the whole playlist, or you can download it at *threadsmedia.com/sacredroads*.

Of the three purposes for reading the Bible, which resonates with you most? What other benefits can you think of?

Given those points, why do you think studying the Bible is so difficult for most of us?

As a way to try out intellectual discipleship, watch the video called "Romans 3:23-24" during your small group discussion. This video will help you see an example of how you can grow in your relationship with Jesus through the process of study. You can also download the video for yourself at *threadsmedia.com/sacredroads*.

There's a great moment in *The Lord of the Rings* when Sam says, "I wonder what sort of tale we've fallen into." When we fall into God's tale, and we see ourselves as part of something bigger, we will begin to truly live the life for which we were created. So how do we fall into this tale?

How to Study the Bible
Some people approach the Bible like a roulette wheel, plopping it open and reading wherever it happens to fall. Others look at it like a yearbook, only stopping at their favorite pictures over and over again. But a systematic approach to Bible study can help you appreciate and take in the full counsel of God while at the same time believing that God does have something to say to you in the pages of His Word.

Which Bible study method have you used in the past? Why?

For a more detailed treatment of how to study the Bible, pick up a copy of *How to Read the Bible for All Its Worth* by Gordon Fee or *How to Study Your Bible* by Kay Arthur.

Why do you think it's important to have a systematic approach to Bible study?

Step 1: Choose an appropriate translation.
Finding a good Bible can be intimidating because there are so many. But let me give you a quick course in Bible translation. This is overly-simplified, but there are four main ways to translate the Bible.

One is the literal translation or "formal equivalence." Translations like this attempt to translate the ancient text into our language word by word. It is a straight translation with no concern for sentence structure, figures of speech, euphemisms, or old units of measurements (like spans and homers). They are accurate but not very readable.

"Dynamic equivalence," or thought-for-thought translation, strives to strike a balance between accuracy and readability by translating words, idioms, and grammatical constructions of the original language into precise equivalents in the modern language.

Most of the scriptural references included in this study are from the Holman Christian Standard Bible. Its translators used a method called "optimal equivalence," which seeks to combine the best of word-for-word translation and dynamic equivalence translation.

A free translation, or a paraphrase, attempts to translate the ideas from one language to another without much concern for using the exact words of the original. They are readable but not necessarily accurate.

It's good to use several translations side by side because it gives better perspective on the text. You can do this very easily online at *biblegateway.com* or *youversion.com*.

Step 2: Read critically.

Remember the Bereans? Strive to be like them. Remember that Luke commended them in Acts 17 for their careful thought and consideration of the Word of God. If we want to really mine the depths of the Bible, we should follow the three-step process of observation, interpretation, and application, asking ourselves critical questions during our reading.

Observation: What does the text say?

During the observation process, you'll want to find out who the author and audience are, along with the purpose and timing of the book. As you keep those key pieces of information in mind, you can move further into the study, doing things like breaking the book into sections based on main ideas and eventually individual verses. Be sure and record what you've done because chances are, you won't remember.

Interpretation: What does the text mean?

In this step of Bible study, you take all that information you accumulated during observation and try and isolate the meaning. To do so, you'll need to ask even more questions: What is the literary

Examples of formal equivalence translations include the New American Standard and the King James Version. The New International Version is a good example of a dynamic equivalence translation, while The Living Bible and *The Message* are examples of free translations.

structure (poetry, Law, history, epistle)? What is the historical setting (time period, war, peace, exile, etc.)? What is the cultural context?

Always allow Scripture to interpret Scripture. If the passage is difficult to understand, cross-reference it with other verses in Scripture that speak to the same topic. And again, take notes.

Application: How does the text practically apply to my life today?
D. L. Moody said, "The Bible was not given to increase our knowledge but to change our lives."[25] The intentional application of the Scripture to our lives is where we want to get to. If we accumulate all the knowledge in the world but our lives never change, our study of Scripture is incomplete and will only lead to pride. During the observation and interpretation phases, we place Scripture under the microscope of reason. During the application phase, we place our lives under the microscope of Scripture.

One of my mentors, Dave Buehring, has always encouraged me to apply Scripture by identifying a SPECK of truth each time I read:

- Sin to confess?
- Promise to claim?
- Example to follow?
- Command to obey?
- Knowledge of God to believe?

Finally, write down what you observe, what you have learned, and how you will apply it.

> **Which of the three steps do you think is easiest? Which one is the most difficult? Why?**

THEOLOGICAL STUDY
"Theology" is derived from two Greek words: *Theos* (God) and *logos* (speech or reason). Theology in its simplest terms is rational discussion about God. If we have ever talked about or thought about God, we are theologians. Therefore, whether we want to be or not, all of us are theologians. The question is, are you a good theologian?

Don't have a theological library to help you in your study of Scripture? Not to worry—check out *studylight.org, crosswalk.com,* and *lifeway.com/bible* for free online Bible study tools.

Paul encouraged the church at Ephesus to grow in their thoughts and understanding of their faith:

"Then we will no longer be little children, tossed by the waves and blown around by every wind of teaching, by human cunning with cleverness in the techniques of deceit" (Ephesians 4:14).

Many people try to avoid theology or downplay its importance with various arguments—it kills the simple joy of faith; it's divisive; it's useless speculation; theology hasn't been settled for 2,000 years so there's no difference we can make; you get the idea. Problem is, all of those arguments are theological statements in and of themselves.

What objections have you had in the past (and perhaps now) concerning the study of theology? Is there any validity to some of these objections?

Systematic theology typically seeks to organize ideas about faith around seven basic topics—God, humanity, Jesus, the Holy Spirit, the church, eschatology (the end times), and the Scriptures. Growing into maturity means having biblical thoughts about each of these areas. Thinking correctly about these areas grounds our lives in biblical, proven truths, moving us from a blind faith to an informed faith. And for many people, studying theology makes them love God more.

First Timothy 6:3 says that the teachings of Christ are the foundation for a godly life. The more we know about God and His ways, the more we can trust Him, praise Him, and tell others about Him. It's important because the way we think affects the way we act, and right thinking leads to right action. As Paul said in Titus 2:1, "Promote the kind of living that reflects wholesome teaching" (NLT).

In the book *Who Needs Theology?*, Stanley Grenz asserts, "The question of God is implied in all of life's ultimate questions. Whenever and wherever a person reflects on the great 'Why?' questions of life, at least indirect reflection on or toward God is involved. God is the horizon of all human wondering. This means that in amazing ways even popular authors, composers, playwrights, poets, and creators of pop culture function as theologians."[26]

B. B. Warfield promoted a classic definition of theology as follows: "Theology is the science of God and His relationship to man and the world." In greater detail, theology is the "discipline which 1) presents a unified formulation of truth concerning God and His relationship to humanity and the universe as this is set forth in divine revelation and that 2) applies such truths to the entire range of human thought and life" (from *Evangelical Dictionary of Theology*, second edition, p. 1162).

Visit any church's Web site and you'll find a page of "what we believe" statements. At the bare minimum, you'll find the church's stance on the seven basic topics of systematic theology.

The Institutes of the Christian Religion by John Calvin is generally regarded as one of the most complete and finest systematic theologies ever written. It's a great resource to read, but be prepared—it's divided into four separate books and most translations come in at more than 1500 pages.

One of the more contemporary systematic theologies was written by Wayne Grudem. *Systematic Theology: An Introduction to Biblical Doctrine* is required reading at many Bible colleges and seminaries.

Here are some resources for your library as suggested by Stanley Grenz in *Who Needs Theology*?

1. A good study Bible.

2. A one-volume Bible commentary.

3. A Bible dictionary or encyclopedia.

4. A concordance.

5. An encyclopedia of church history.

6. An encyclopedia of theology.

7. A copy of the historical creeds and confessions of the faith from various traditions.

8. A copy of your own church's or denomination's statement of faith.

Do you agree or disagree with this statement by Grenz? Who are some contemporary creators of pop culture acting as theologians today?

Are their views of God consistent or inconsistent with Scripture?

Grenz identified three characteristics of a good theologian: 1) being more interested in God Himself than merely in thoughts about God, 2) dissatisfaction with your current level of understanding, and 3) willingness to work. Which of those three areas are you strongest in? Which are you weakest in?

Here are some practical steps to continue your theological education:

1. Read a basic systematic theology textbook. Ask your pastor for some recommendations.
2. Read a book that explores a single topic from several perspectives.
3. Sign up for a theology class at a local university or seminary. If your church offers a class, take it first.
4. Always engage in theological study with a group of friends who love God and are pursuing it for the purpose of becoming more like Him.
5. Pick out one theologian in history and read as much as you can by and about him or her.

Have you ever considered yourself to be a theologian? Do you now? How can you become a better theologian?

DARE TO EXPLORE

You might be one idea away from a total transformation, the breaking of a sinful habit, or a new sense of awe and wonder that leads to worship. Intellectual discipleship is not about a cold, academic gathering of facts or mental assent to a set of theological propositions. Rather, it's about changing the way you live by changing the way you think. It's about rediscovering the life-changing power of the Bible, building on a solid theological foundation, and being sure of what you believe. But like all the discipleship methods we've studied so far, there are potential problems and pitfalls you should look out for as you explore.

First, make sure you're more interested in knowing God than in gathering facts about God. Knowing God leads to spiritual growth. Knowing facts about God without a developing relationship with Him can lead only to pride. The pitfall many people get trapped in is knowing and not doing. In the Hebrew mindset, there was no difference between knowing and doing. In our culture, which draws heavily on the Greek mindset, we have created a distinction between intellectual knowledge and practical application. Sometimes we become so entrenched in our study that we forget why we study—to become more like Christ.

Secondly, take care to not get stuck in controversy. I love a good debate, and find that I learn and grow as a result. But sometimes we just get stuck in argument for argument's sake. Make sure you remain involved in a community of relational discipleship and the outward expressions of service, or incarnational discipleship, to avoid unproductive and ungodly debates.

> **What other problems and pitfalls might be related to intellectual discipleship if taken too far or pursued at the exclusion of other methods?**

"He that studies only men, will get the body of knowledge without the soul; and he that studies only books, the soul without the body. He that to what he sees, adds observation, and to what he reads, reflection, is in the right road to knowledge."[27]
—Caleb Colton

ANOTHER VOICE—ANOTHER ERA
DALLAS WILLARD (1935–)

Dallas Willard, a professor in the School of Philosophy at the University of Southern California, is a modern-day intellectual disciple and disciple-maker. In his book *Renovation of the Heart*, he asserts, "It is in our thoughts that the first movements toward the renovation of the heart occur."[28]

Willard received bachelor's degrees from Tennessee Temple College (psychology) and Baylor University (philosophy and religion) and his Ph.D. from the University of Wisconsin (major in philosophy and minor in the history of science). His primary interests of study and teaching are in the areas of epistemology (thinking about how we think), the philosophy of mind and logic, and the philosophy of Edmund Husserl (German philosopher credited as the founder of phenomenology). Willard's books *Renovation of the Heart* and *The Divine Conspiracy* have spurred thousands of Christians to think more deeply about their faith and the way they practically live it out in their day-to-day lives. Like Paul, he is competing with the culture and fighting for the faith in the academic community, the Areopagus of our day.

TRY IT OUT

Memorize Romans 12:2: *"Do not be conformed to this age, but be transformed by the renewing of your mind, so that you may discern what is the good, pleasing, and perfect will of God."*

Read Psalm 101 and identify a SPECK of truth.

• *S (Sin to confess?)*

• *P (Promise to claim?)*

• *E (Example to follow?)*

• *C (Command to obey?)*

• *K (Knowledge of God to believe?)*

session four
Personal Discipleship

Nikolaus sat in his study, poring over his diary entries from the past six months:

February 1: "...a very blessed night in which in deep humility before His presence I prayed for everyone in Herrnhut by name."

March 9: "...spoke earnestly with our servant Christoph and was deeply humbled by his testimony...he is far in advance of me."

April 14: (Melchoir's death.) "This gave me an opportunity to examine my own heart."

Nikolaus was thankful that his grandmother's friend, the Pietist minister, had encouraged him to write down the discoveries, successes, and weaknesses of his spiritual life. It gave him an opportunity to connect the dots, to see more clearly the hand of God in his life.

He had provided refuge for hundreds of persecuted religious people. He had published books to encourage their spiritual progress. A 24-hour prayer chain started two years ago was still going strong. But none of it mattered if his heart was not properly organized. Tonight would be another opportunity to examine his heart, to make sure it was governed by God.

Just then, David's face popped into the window. Christian followed behind. Nikolaus stepped outside to greet his two friends. He once dreaded these regular meetings, but he had grown to anticipate them. They met not to talk about politics or current affairs, but about their hearts. More specifically, what remained in their lives that marred the image of Christ. They took turns sharing, confessing, and encouraging. It was painful but also uplifting. And it had become an activity that they regularly looked forward to.

Count Nikolaus von Zinzendorf juggled the obligations of nobility and the calling of God to shepherd the Moravian movement, which rejected the intellectualism of the Protestant Reformation in favor of inward piety and spiritual transformation.

THE QUIET TIME

Begrudgingly, I rolled out of bed and headed toward the church. In all my sixth grade defiance, I acquiesced to the expectation of Vacation Bible School attendance, but I wasn't happy about it. Vacation Bible School? For sixth graders? Seriously? Who even knew such a thing existed?

As I sat on the red carpeted floor of the aptly named "Red Room," I listened to youth leaders expound upon principle after principle of the Christian life. I'm sure many insightful and valuable things were said that week, but one thing stuck out in particular and shaped my life in significant ways.

Confessions by Augustine is the recording of the thoughts, prayers, and journals of one of Christianity's most formative figures. Pick it up to read about what led to his conversion and get a glimpse into the devotional life of one of church history's greatest figures.

Marti Pulliam, who I had already grown to respect and admire, casually talked about a practice that had changed her life—the daily quiet time. Most of the time, ideas grow on me slowly, but right then, I decided to start doing what Marti described. I didn't really have any idea what I was doing or how to do it (I'm sure Marti covered that but I probably got distracted by the eighth grade boy across the room), but I figured it had something to do with reading my Bible and praying. So that's what I started doing.

In recent years, I've found the value, once again, of scaling back to the simple but significant time alone with God. I'm also slowly discovering that the world is noisy, and sometimes we need to heed the advice we learned in kindergarten—stop, look, and listen. It's the practice of personal discipleship—the spiritual disciplines, time carved out for God, and the intentional ordering of our lives—that often spurs us on to greater spiritual growth.

GROWING IN FAITH THROUGH PERSONAL DISCIPLINE

Up until the 19th and 20th centuries, the focus of religious life was on the community. The church was the people of God, and spirituality was thought of in terms of "together." But in the 1800s a new emphasis on personal conversion came to the surface. For the first time, phrases like "personal relationship with Christ" and "quiet time" started being used with regularity. And the emphasis on a personal relationship with Christ propelled a shift to a personal approach to discipleship.

The church moved from a state institution to small fellowships of people who had experienced personal conversions to Christ; and the church provided those people with personal growth resources and taught them how to develop their relationships with God. People

74

grew in their knowledge and relationship with God through personal discipline and time alone with Him.

Do you currently have a regular time alone with God? If so, in what specific ways is that practice helping you grow in your relationship with Christ?

The lyrics to the hymn "Abide with Me" capture the essence of the personal approach to discipleship:

"Swift to its close ebbs out life's little day; Earths' joys grow dim, its glories pass away; Change and decay in all around I see; O Thou who changes not, abide with me."

Do you tend to grow best within the context of community or alone?

What aspects of your spiritual growth are impacted more by being in community? By being alone?

The hymn "Abide with Me," which was sung at the wedding of Queen Elizabeth II, was written in 1847 by Henry Francis Lyte as he was dying of tuberculosis. Required to seek a warmer climate in Italy for health reasons, he lived by the philosophy, "It is better to wear out than to rust out."

PIETISTS, PURITANS, AND PUBLISHING HOUSES

Though the desert fathers and spiritual mystics of the early centuries of the church established the practical foundations for personal discipleship, its modern origins can be traced back to the Pietist movement. That movement began within 70 years of the Reformation as a reaction against the intellectualism of Luther's ideas. The Pietists focused on personal Bible study and prayer and encouraged the experience of an inward and heartfelt Christian life as opposed to scholasticism. Pietism stressed the necessity of a personal conversion and shifted the center of the Christian experience from state churches

Count Nikolaus von Zinzendorf spearheaded the Moravian movement, which sought a "heart" faith in contrast to what was perceived as the cold intellectualism of the Reformation. John and Charles Wesley were converted through their contact with the Moravians (John journaled, "I felt my heart strangely warmed") and always held them in high esteem.

In college, Jonathan Edwards drafted a statement of resolutions that included, "Resolved, to live with all my might while I do live." (Check out *apuritansmind.com* to see the complete list of resolutions.) While he lived with great passion and spoke words of great passion, his preaching style was anything but passionate. He wrote out his sermons, held them close to his face, and read them word for word. Observers said he "scarcely gestured" and didn't vary his voice or give particular emphasis to any portions of the text. However, people experienced violent physical and emotional reactions when they heard him preach. "Sinners in the Hands of an Angry God" is his most famous sermon.

to intimate fellowships of people who could give witness to a personal relationship with Christ. The importance of pastoral care replaced the pageantry of the Catholic priesthood and the intellectualism of the pastor-scholar in the Reformation churches.

Some of the leaders of the movement included Philip Jakob Spener, August Hermann Francke, and Count Nikolaus von Zinzendorf. People in the pews were no longer spectators or students, but active participants who ministered to one another in the spirit of 1 Peter 2:9:

"But you are a chosen race, a royal priesthood, a holy nation, a people for His possession, so that you may proclaim the praises of the One who called you out of darkness into His marvelous light."

Then, in the mid-1700s, revivalism swept through America. The preaching of Jonathan Edwards and other Puritan preachers brought conviction, repentance, and the pursuit of personal holiness. While today we often equate Puritanism with words like straight-laced, legalistic, uptight, and, um, boring, its original expression was passionate. The preaching style of the Puritans was aimed at the heart instead of the head.

Another wave of personal discipleship came in the form of fundamentalism. While that word, like Puritanism, carries a lot of baggage with it today, its roots lay in a desire to return to the clear and simple truths of the Scriptures, giving the inner life priority over social concern. In the 1880s and 1890s, Bible study and personal holiness seemed more rewarding than social reform and so many people turned their attention to their inward spiritual lives.

In *Church History in Plain Language*, Shelley describes the phenomenon in this way: "While increased attention both to the end times and to personal Christian living had firm biblical roots, it also gave traditional evangelicals a way of maintaining their faith in a culture over which they were steadily losing control. If they could not shape the affairs of men, they could find comfort in the world of the spirit."[29]

Which is more important, to shape the affairs of culture or to shape our inward lives? Why?

Which do you gravitate toward in your spiritual life? Why?

The result was a privatization of faith—a faith that served the areas of private life like child rearing, family harmony, personal emotions, and the management of finances. The focus on personal devotion created a market for resources, and the development of denomination-based publishing houses soon followed.

Bibles, spiritual growth resources, and studies are now produced in mass in various translations for women, men, leaders, teenagers, teachers, and other groups. All these resources are geared toward being relevant and specific to the needs of the individual as they seek to develop their personal relationships with Christ.

SHEPHERDS, NAZIRITES, AND WAITERS

Throughout the Old Testament, we see God strengthening and forming future leaders in the solitude and quiet places of their lives. Moses, for example, recognized the value of separating himself from people and responsibilities:

"Now Moses took a tent and set it up outside the camp, far away from the camp; he called it the tent of meeting. Anyone who wanted to consult the LORD would go to the tent of meeting that was outside the camp" (Exodus 33:7).

Moses was leading a few million people out of Egypt to the promised land. That's a pretty time-consuming responsibility. But he understood the need to regularly get "outside the camp"—to remove himself from the day-to-day leadership obligations and expectations in order to seek the wisdom and presence of God. So he moved himself a good distance from the rest of the Israelites' dwellings and pitched a tent for the purpose of spending time alone with God.

David understood this as well. As a shepherd, he spent countless hours alone. That's not exactly the standard training ground for a budding warrior-king. I would have picked the firing range or a pee-wee football league. But it was in the pasture that God prepared David for a more important and strategic arena:

The United Methodist Publishing House, known today as Cokesbury (named after Methodist pioneers Thomas Coke and Francis Asbury) was founded in 1789 for the purpose of publishing and distributing resources for the United Methodist Church and the larger Christian community. The Baptist Sunday School Board (now known as Lifeway) was formed in 1891 by James Frost. The Baptist Bookstore, now known as LifeWay Christian Stores, first opened its doors in 1920 and began to sell hymnals, prayer books, Bibles, Sunday School books, Sunday School teachers' manuals, religious books, and other church and personal growth resources.

The Bible contains many references to bears and lions, but they cannot be found in the Holy Land today. They likely vanished from Palestine during the Middle Ages.

"'Don't let anyone be discouraged by him; your servant will go and fight this Philistine . . . Your servant has been tending his father's sheep. Whenever a lion or a bear came and carried off a lamb from the flock, I went after it, struck it down, and rescued the lamb from its mouth. If it reared up against me, I would grab it by its fur, strike it down, and kill it. Your servant has killed lions and bears; this uncircumcised Philistine will be like one of them, for he has defied the armies of the living God.' Then David said, 'The LORD who rescued me from the paw of the lion and the paw of the bear will rescue me from the hand of this Philistine'" (1 Samuel 17:32-37).

In Scripture, it appears that busier people needed more time alone. What is the balance of activity and solitude in your life right now?

In the Old Testament, we also see men and women growing in their relationships with God by living their lives according to a code of principles and discipline. Numbers 6:2-21 introduces a form of ancient spiritual devotion rooted in the observance of a strict regimen of outward spiritual disciplines that reflected an inward reality. The Nazirites expressed their devotion to God by abstaining from wine and strong drink, cutting their hair, and contact with dead people. Some of the Bible's most famous Nazirites include Samson, Samuel, and John the Baptist.

While these men evidently lived according to a lifetime vow, most Nazirite vows lasted between 30 and 100 days and were taken for the purpose of intentional growth for a specific season.

Are there any activities that you have made a decision to control or refrain from in your own life—either for life or for a season—for the purpose of showing devotion to God?

Write down a few phrases that reflect the code of conduct by which you live your life.

As a teenager, Daniel laid a foundation of holiness and integrity that followed him throughout his life. As the pages of Scripture open on Daniel's life, he makes a potentially life-threatening decision to follow the rules of God instead of enjoying the carnivorous buffet in the king's palace. It may not have seemed like a significant decision, but Daniel recognized that small decisions and simple discipline have the potential for tremendous repercussions.

In the sixth and seventh chapters of the Book of Daniel, we see an older man who grew in wisdom and position because of small decisions to remain devoted to God. And he continued to practice those disciplines.

> **Read Daniel 1. What were the potential dangers of Daniel's decision? What factors may have helped him commit to that decision? What were the results?**

> **Read Daniel 6 and 7. What else can we learn about Daniel's personal discipline from these passages? How do you think the foundation he laid in Daniel 1 prepared him for these experiences?**

Another personal discipline the Old Testament encourages is the practice of waiting on the Lord. The Book of Psalms encourages the reader seven times to wait on the Lord. Consider the words of the prophets Isaiah and Jeremiah that further the discipline of waiting:

"Lᴏʀᴅ, be gracious to us! We wait for You. Be our strength every morning, and our salvation in time of trouble" (Isaiah 33:2).

"Because of the Lᴏʀᴅ's faithful love we do not perish, for His mercies never end. They are new every morning; great is Your faithfulness! I say: The Lᴏʀᴅ is my portion, therefore I will put my hope in Him. The Lᴏʀᴅ is good to those who wait for Him, to the person who seeks Him. It is good to wait quietly for deliverance from the Lᴏʀᴅ. It is good for a man to bear the yoke while he is still young. Let him sit alone and be silent, for God has disciplined him" (Lamentations 3:22-28).

The first seven chapters of the Book of Daniel are devoted to recounting the story of his life. The final seven chapters contain the images of his apocalyptic vision.

Daniel 5 highlights one of the strange circumstances that surrounded the life of Daniel. King Belshazzar threw a party one night, and during the celebration a hand started writing on the palace wall. David was summoned to interpret the writing, and this was the message delivered to the king: "Your days are numbered. You have failed the test. Your kingdom will be divided." What happened to this messenger of bad news? Belshazzar promoted him to the third highest position in the land and gave him a new wardrobe.

The Book of Lamentations is a collection of five poems penned by the prophet Jeremiah after the fall of Jerusalem in 587 B.C. The first four poems are acrostics, in which each verse begins with a different letter of the Hebrew alphabet in successive order.

Describe a time when you had to wait on God for something. What did you learn in the process?

Listen to the audio segment called "Experimenting with Personal Discipleship" this week. Your group leader will send it to you via e-mail, or you can download it at *threadsmedia.com/sacredroads*. These audio recordings are designed to help you connect with different expressions of discipleship.

How do you know when you should wait on God and when God is waiting on you to act?

JESUS' PERSONAL SPIRITUALITY

In Mark 1:35, we read that "Very early in the morning, while it was still dark, Jesus got up, left the house and went off to a solitary place, where He prayed" (NIV). In Luke 5:16 we read, "But Jesus often withdrew to the wilderness for prayer" (NLT). And in Matthew 14:23, "After dismissing the crowds, He went up on the mountain by Himself to pray. When evening came, He was there alone" (HCSB). Jesus knew the importance of the quiet time.

Jesus was constantly seeking out solitude for prayer—before He chose His disciples, after the beheading of John the Baptist, and before going to the cross. In fact, it seems Jesus slipped away from the crowds at His most popular or most life-changing moments. Here's the thought that keeps coming back to me: If Jesus prayed this much, then how much more do I need to pray?

Jesus lived in such an intimate relationship with His heavenly Father that He said He only spoke and acted according to what the Father instructed Him to say and do. And in Matthew 6, Jesus taught and demonstrated how we should interact with the Father through prayer. He also addressed how our inward life should affect the practical areas of our personal lives.

If Jesus is God, why was it important that He seek times of solitude and invest time in prayer?

Read Matthew 6. What can we learn from Jesus' teaching on the following subjects:

• **Service?**

• **Prayer?**

• **Fasting?**

• **Integrity?**

• **Trust?**

Matthew 6 is part of the Sermon on the Mount, the longest of Jesus' sermons recorded in Scripture. For a great, in-depth book on the implications of the sermon, read *The Divine Conspiracy* by Dallas Willard.

PERSONAL DISCIPLESHIP IN THE NEW TESTAMENT

The early church learned from Jesus' example of a personal, private devotional life. Prayer was the catalyst of change in the Book of Acts. The Holy Spirit came on those who prayed (Acts 2). Prayer set the stage for the spread of the gospel to the Gentiles (Acts 10:9). The leaders of the early church began everything with prayer and they depended on prayer. Their ministry flowed out of their prayer lives. I think I sometimes get it backwards. I tend to pray in order for God to bless my purpose in life. The early leaders prayed in order to discover their purpose in life.

In *Streams of Living Water*, Richard Foster offers the apostle James, the brother of Jesus, as an example of one who seeks spiritual growth through a process of action stemming from personal conviction and conversion. Eusebius records that James "used to enter alone into the temple and be found kneeling and praying for forgiveness for the people, so that his knees grew hard like a camel's because of his constant worship of God."[30]

In 1 Corinthians 9:25-27, Paul, too, got in on personal discipleship, comparing spiritual development to physical training:

"Now everyone who competes exercises self-control in everything. However, they do it to receive a perishable crown, but we an imperishable one. Therefore I do not run like one who runs aimlessly, or box like one

Paul was fond of using athletic metaphors in his writing. Check out these other passages where he employs the symbolism:
  • Galatians 5:7
  • Philippians 3:13-14
  • 2 Timothy 2:5

who beats the air. Instead, I discipline my body and bring it under strict control, so that after preaching to others, I myself will not be disqualified" (1 Corinthians 9:25-27).

> What are some practical applications of Paul's metaphor?

> What are some of the obstacles in your own life to pursuing that kind of discipline?

PUTTING IT INTO PRACTICE

Applications of personal discipleship include the practice of daily quiet times, the development of personal spiritual disciplines, and the establishment of a rule of life.

QUIET TIMES

Too Busy Not to Pray by Bill Hybels echoes a similar sentiment to Martin Luther. Hybels offers practical suggestions of how to integrate a quiet time focused on prayer into the life of someone who is perpetually "too busy."

The great reformer Martin Luther said, "I have so much business I cannot get on without spending three hours daily in prayer."[31] Luther was a pretty busy man—defending his theology, translating the Bible into German, writing books, and leading a Reformation—so I imagine he spent several days in three-hour prayer. How I wish I were more like Luther! Instead of following Luther's example and praying more on my crazy days, I tend to pray less.

The quiet time might mean different things to different people, but I would define it as the time you carve out of your schedule to connect with God every day. For me, this typically consists of reading, praying, and journaling. Some additional spiritual disciplines—solitude, silence, and simplicity—generally accompany the quiet time. Other spiritual disciplines like fasting or confession are often completely different spiritual practices. There is no hard line between these categories nor should there be. The most important aspect of the quiet time is intentionality.

John Ortberg said, "The great danger is not that we will renounce our faith. It is that we will become so distracted and rushed and preoccupied that we will settle for a mediocre version of it. We will just skim our lives instead of actually living them."[32]

Remember Moses and his tent? I don't know a whole lot about tents, but I know it takes a little time and effort to get the thing up. But once it's up, the tent becomes an important place of rest and retreat. Sometimes, it takes an initial investment of discipline to create places of rest. That's what time with God does for us. Spending time alone in our tent with God is a time for rest and recharging of our spiritual batteries.

But the tent also protects us from the elements. Listen to the Psalmist:

"Hear my cry, O God; listen to my prayer. From the ends of the earth I call to you, I call as my heart grows faint; lead me to the rock that is higher than I. For you have been my refuge, a strong tower against the foe. I long to dwell in your tent forever and take refuge in the shelter of your wings" (Psalm 61:1-4, NIV).

Maybe you have a hard time setting a time and place for a regular meeting with God. You feel like sometimes it's more trouble and stress than it's worth. But once it becomes a habit, it's something you look forward to. So here are some practical steps to developing a quiet time:

1. Schedule it. For most of us, we actually have to build time for God into the calendar. Make it a blocked off time just like any other appointment or meeting. And just as you would any other meeting, guard that time because it's spoken for.

2. Pick a place. There's something about having a specific place set aside for time with God that causes a shift in mindset. Every time you come to that place, you are reminded of what happens there.

3. Have a plan. What will you read? How will you pray? Will you journal? If you take time to answer these questions, then you can really make the most of your set aside time.

4. Change it up. Even though the regularity of the time and place is good, changing the actual process is a really healthy thing. Sing. Read. Just listen. Keep the variety and you'll continually have something to look forward to.

Does the idea of a personal quiet time seem like an exercise of rest or an exercise of obligation? Does it seem like a place of safety or a place of duty?

One of the best known and most widely read devotional books is *My Utmost for His Highest* by Oswald Chambers. You can read the book or search through it by day or Scripture text at *myutmost.org*.

To find a Bible reading plan to use as a part of your quiet time, visit *bibleplan.org*. You can find a plan that will allow you to read the whole Bible in a year, focus on the New Testament, focus on the Old Testament, or read the Scriptures chronologically.

Record how the following passages affect your thinking:

- Psalm 46:10

- Psalm 61:1-4

- John 15:1-17

- 1 Corinthians 9:25-27

SPIRITUAL DISCIPLINES

I spent many hours of my freshman year of high school running up and down the bleachers of Murphy High School. Up and down. Over and over again. The ritual went on for hours. Days. Weeks. What would lead an otherwise normal and smart young high school student to engage in such a stupid and seemingly pointless ritual?

Track team. 400-meter run.

I hated it, but in every sport I played, we were forced to participate in stupid drills. I wanted to just get out on the court or field and play, but my coaches kept forcing us to do all these silly, pointless exercises. As I matured, however, I realized I couldn't play the game without the drills. They weren't pointless. They were designed to make us stronger, quicker, and more intuitive. They made us people of instinct. Drills prepared us for the game.

I think spiritual disciplines are like athletic drills. Prayer, fasting, meditation, journaling, and other disciplines are the elements of life that make us strong, fast, and ready. Honestly, sometimes I've wondered if God commanded us to do them just to keep us off the streets. But when I encounter the tense, painful, and important moments in the game of life, I realize that spiritual disciplines, like athletic drills, are not meant to just keep me busy. In 1 Timothy 4:7-8, Paul wrote about the goal of spiritual drills:

"But have nothing to do with irreverent and silly myths. Rather, train yourself in godliness, for, the training of the body has a limited benefit, but godliness is beneficial in every way, since it holds promise for the present life and also for the life to come."

The bleachers at the Murphy High School track caught on fire and burned to the ground in 1990, one year after Heather left the track team. They have yet to be rebuilt.

Richard Foster, the best known Quaker of today, wrote the landmark book *Celebration of Discipline*. It has sold more than one million copies and was recognized by *Christianity Today* as one of the most influential books of the 20th century. In the book, Foster categorized the disciplines into inward, outward, and corporate, and provides practical examples of how to implement them into our spiritual lives.

Spiritual drills prepare me to play to the best of my ability. They train me into Christ-likeness. The disciplines and the drills are not the goals; rather, they are the preparation to attaining the ultimate goal. Let's take a look at some of these time-tested exercises of the faith.

Fasting

In *A Discipleship Journey*, Dave Buehring defines fasting as "setting aside food (or another life necessity or pleasure) to focus on prayer and seeking God's face."[33] John Wesley required his pastors to fast twice a week. Thomas à Kempis believed that the value of fasting was that it brought the entire life under control: "Summon up your inner resources to resist the devil's evil assaults, curb your appetite, and you will be better able to keep under the unruly desires of the flesh."[34]

There is nothing magical or formulaic about fasting, but those who have incorporated it into their lives point to a number of ways that the practice spurs spiritual growth. Fasting helps us realign our lives, overcome sinful habits, hear from God, and intensify our focus in prayer. But how? Like anything else, it's good to have a plan when you walk into a fast.

Various types and purposes of fasts are mentioned in both the Old Testament (Leviticus 23:26-32; 1 Samuel 1:1-20; 2 Chronicles 20; Ezra 8; Esther 4; Daniel 2; Jonah 3) and the New Testament (Matthew 6:17-18; Luke 4; Jesus' wilderness temptation; Acts 14). Fasts were done for a variety of reasons, including intercession, repentance, seeking guidance, and commissioning into ministry. Some fasts lasted a short period of time; others lasted up to 40 days.

1. Determine your purpose for the fast. It could be to establish a new regular discipline of fasting, to incorporate a new spiritual discipline like prayer or meditation during a time you would normally eat, to seek specific guidance from God, or to overcome a sinful habit. Regardless, know why you're doing what you're doing.
2. Decide the extent of your fast—what you will fast from and for how long. If you've never fasted before, begin small. You might try to fast from food from dinner to dinner, or from television for a day.
3. Find someone to hold you accountable and ensure your health.
4. Add other disciplines, such as prayer, Scripture meditation, and journaling in order to process and learn from your time.
5. Plan a time of celebration at the end of the fast. From personal experience, I would encourage you to avoid pizza and hamburgers at the celebration meal.

> **Fasting in Scripture is always related to the abstinence from food, but we often fast from other things, too (television, computer, music, etc.). Is fasting from food superior to other forms of fasts? Why or why not?**

Can you think of any reason(s) why food fasts might be unique in their ability to help us grow spiritually?

Prayer

The daily quiet time is the environment in which we tend to think about prayer. And though it's good to prioritize a specific time of prayer each day, prayer could also be defined as a growing consciousness of God. *The Message* translation of 1 Peter 1:17 says, "Your life is a journey you must travel with a deep consciousness of God."

Is it possible to have a prayer life that saturates your entire day? Is it possible to journey through your day with ongoing thoughts about God? Can you truly "pray constantly" in compliance with the command in 1 Thessalonians 5:17?

Brother Lawrence, a 17th-century monk, set a seemingly impossible goal—to attain a life of on-going, ceaseless prayer. He sought to accomplish this by viewing every single action of his day as an expression of prayer. Whether he washed dishes, ate, cleaned, or worked in the garden, he endeavored to turn those small acts into moments of devotion, prayer, and worship.

Likewise, the Benedictine Order of monks incorporated prayer into their daily chores. Before starting a new task and throughout the process, they would pray, "O God, make speed to save me, O Lord make haste to help me." I'm going to remember that one the next time I'm scrubbing the toilet or heading into a rough meeting. At the end of a task, they would pray, "Blessed are you, O Lord, my God, for you help me and strengthen me."

Write out a specific prayer to be said during each of the following:
• Waking up in the morning

• Before starting work

Brother Lawrence's experiments in prayer and worship were recorded in his book *The Practice of the Presence of God.*

• **When eating lunch**

• **When first laying in bed at night**

Journaling

When I was in engineering school, I was forced to draw everything in my notebook. Whatever I saw under the microscope, I had to draw. I hated that. I don't have an artistic bone in my body, and I found the practice embarrassing and useless . . . until exam time rolled around. That's when I appreciated all those drawing assignments. I recognized that because I was forced to draw, I was forced to look more carefully. Drawing the specimen helped me see it better. I think the same thing happens when we journal. The process of writing things out helps us recognize and acknowledge the hand of God at work in our lives and thus journaling itself becomes an act of worship.

Many people are thankful that the Scriptures never say, "And Jesus withdrew to the wilderness to journal." Granted, we don't see the clear instruction to journal as we do with other disciplines like prayer, fasting, and confession. But that doesn't mean that there is not biblical precedent. After all, the Bible itself is the result of men who took the time to write down the events of their lives, the work of God in their day, and their emotions, reactions, questions, and gratitude.

Journaling is important because it helps us remember what we've learned, it helps us see more of the work of God around us, and it helps us measure the movement toward Christ in our lives. Here are some ideas to help you get started:

1. Pick a specific style of journaling to experiment with: daily log of activities, prayer, Bible reading, gratitude, or spiritual observations.
2. Pick the right notebook. Some people need to invest in a nice journal to make them more diligent and devoted to the practice. Nice notebooks paralyze me because I feel the need to write something profound. So I prefer the plain, one-subject, spiral bound varieties.
3. Discipline yourself to record at least once a day. Good times are in the morning when you first wake up or at night.
4. Change it up. Don't write everyday. Try drawing, pasting in photographs, or quoting someone from a book. This kind of variety will keep the process of journaling fresh.

The Psalms are basically praise and prayers captured from the journals of people like Moses, Asaph, and David. Lamentations is a journal containing Jeremiah's reflections on the fall of Jerusalem. And the Hebrew people journaled their story over and over. Deuteronomy is a re-telling of Exodus, Leviticus, and Numbers, and the Books of 1 and 2 Chronicles are a re-telling of 2 Samuel through 2 Kings.

St. Benedict organized much of his monastic rule around the discipline of silence.

Solitude, Silence, and Stillness

The Israelites were backed into a corner. The Red Sea was in front of them. The Egyptian army was chasing them. And they began to complain. In Exodus 14:13-14, Moses answered the people:

"Don't be afraid. Stand firm and see the Lord's salvation He will provide for you today; for the Egyptians you see today, you will never see again. The Lord will fight for you; you must be quiet."

The NIV translation says, "You need only to be still." Why does God's plan always seem so counterintuitive? Think about it—be still when logic tells you to run away from the army trying to kill you. Maybe God knows that true strength is found in quiet dependence upon Him instead of our frantic striving.

Technically, solitude, silence, and stillness are three separate practices. But to me, they are intimately related. Abraham Lincoln once said, "Better to remain silent and be thought a fool than to speak out and remove all doubt."[35] Perhaps that's why James instructed us to "be quick to hear, slow to speak, and slow to anger" (James 1:19). He also commented that true religion and the ability to control the tongue were interconnected (James 1:26).

What's the purpose of these disciplines? First and foremost, solitude, silence, and stillness remove the distractions, reduce the noise, and clear the clutter of our lives. In so doing, we are able to hear God more clearly. The second purpose, which is actually a result of the first, is that our minds would be renewed and our hearts realigned with God's.

These three disciplines fit together in this manner: solitude facilitates the practice of stillness and silence. If you're ready to be quiet for a while, try these steps to getting there:

1. Pick a time and place.
2. Remove all distractions.
3. Be quiet and listen to God for two minutes.
4. Locate a local monastery that would allow you to participate in a silent retreat.

> **Be quiet and listen to God for two minutes. When you are done, write down how you felt during the experience. Did the time pass quickly or slowly?**

The Book of James is one of the most practical in the entire Bible. James wrote to encourage a suffering congregation to let their actions line up with their faith, and that if that doesn't happen, their faith is worthless.

Listen to "How Deep the Father's Love for Us" by Kendall Payne from the *Sacred Roads* playlist. Your group leader can e-mail you the whole playlist, or you can download it at *threadsmedia.com/sacredroads*.

Meditation

William Wilberforce was a member of the English Parliament from 1784–1812 and was primarily responsible for the end of England's participation in the slave trade. While walking between his home and Parliament, he memorized and meditated on Psalm 119. By the end of his life, he could recite the entire psalm by memory.

In the previous session, we focused on the method of Bible study—the academic process of surgically dissecting Scripture so that we can properly understand and apply it. When we study, we place Scripture under the microscope of reason. But there is another way of engaging the Scriptural text—meditation. Psalm 77:11-12 reflects this practice:

"I will remember the LORD's works; yes, I will remember Your ancient wonders. I will reflect on all You have done and meditate on Your actions."

We need to practice both study and meditation, using both reason and revelation. But meditation is flipping studying on its head. Instead of placing Scripture under the microscope, we place our lives under the microscope of Scripture and let it dissect us. John Ortberg said, "The goal is not for us to get through the Scriptures. The goal is to get the Scriptures through us."[36]

Though meditation might sound mystical, it's really a pretty simple process to integrate in your life:

1. Set aside several minutes and find a quiet place. Remove all distractions. Maybe play some quiet worship music.
2. Select a small passage of Scripture and read it through several times.
3. Use your imagination to experience what you're reading. What are the sights? Sounds? Smells? If it's a narrative passage, put yourself into the action. If it's non-narrative, what metaphors, figures of speech, and imagery are being used that can help you more fully understand the text?
4. Emphasize different words each time you read it to grasp every possible nuance.
5. Circle the words that jump out to you.
6. Turn the text into a prayer.

Rule of Life

Obviously, the most difficult part of the spiritual disciplines is putting them into practice. It's very easy to be overwhelmed when getting started. Maybe you try practicing all the disciplines at once and grow

In *Celebration of Discipline*, Richard Foster distinguishes Christian meditation from the form of meditation observed in Eastern religions. He states, "Eastern meditation is an attempt to empty the mind; Christian meditation is an attempt to fill the mind. The two ideas are quite different."[37]

discouraged in your inability to do them, or you become paralyzed by how far you fall short and never try them at all. Establishing a personal rule of life can help you intentionally and strategically integrate these disciplines into your life.

Monastic communities established a rule of life by which its members would abide. The Rule of St. Benedict, written in the seventh century, is one of the most popular. It covers instructions on the practice of worship attendance, daily prayer times, and work habits.

A rule of life is simply a structure that facilitates spiritual formation practices; it puts into words the priorities of the Christian life and focuses on living a life that is intentional and ordered for the purpose of growth and transformation. Basically, it's about setting goals for spiritual disciplines.

If the word "rule" seems too legalistic, then think in terms of "rhythm of life." Or use Dallas Willard's language of "Curriculum of Christlikeness" or John Ortberg's description of a "Game Plan for Morphing." At NCC, we call it a "Spiritual Development Plan."

A rule of life incorporates the right disciplines into the right seasons. It might include things like a 10-day fast at the beginning of each year, reading the entire Bible in a year, meditating on Psalm 119 over the course of a month, or praying each morning, noon, and night. The possibilities are endless and the rule of life will be as unique as you are. Here are some guidelines for creating your own personal rule of life:

1. Take a sheet of paper and create four categories—daily, weekly, monthly, and annual (see chart).
2. Set spiritual discipline goals for each of those categories.
3. Make your goals S.M.A.R.T.—specific, measurable, achievable, requiring faith, and time-related.
4. At the end of six months, conduct a self-assessment to check your progress in practicing the disciplines, but more importantly to evaluate how you are growing—in the fruit of the Spirit, in your ability to hear God, and in the way you relate to other people. Make changes to your rule as necessary.

Devotional Classics edited by Richard Foster is a collection of readings written by some of the foremost historical Christian figures, with commentary written by Foster. Pick up a copy to connect with the inward thoughts of some of the fathers and mothers of the Christian faith.

DARE TO EXPLORE

The development of spiritual disciplines in your life and an intentional strategy for personal growth will provide a foundation that enhances all other forms of discipleship you experience. But once again, there are also some dangers with personal discipleship to look out for along the way.

The focus on inward development may tempt you to dodge social responsibility in the name of personal discipleship. As you will explore in the next session, the great Pietists like Zinzendorf and Francke avoided this trap; they allowed their inward transformation to find outward expressions of love in their work with the poor.

Also, be careful about devaluing intellectual discipleship and neglecting community with other believers. Proverbs says that wisdom is found when we surround ourselves with wise counsel.

What other problems and pitfalls might be related to personal discipleship if taken too far or pursued to the exclusion of other methods?

Personal discipleship has the ability to help you live with great purpose and great depth. But you have to make the choice to do it. You have to choose to get up early, separate yourself, and live with discipline. It's not an easy choice, and it's certainly one that has to be made over and over again—and yet a deep life with Jesus is worth it.

Thomas à Kempis, the great author and thinker concerning faith development, said, "All can not use one kind of spiritual exercise, but one is more beneficial for this person, another for that. Different exercises are also more appropriate for different times [of life]."

ANOTHER VOICE—ANOTHER ERA
PACHOMIUS (292–346)

Pachomius was born in Thebes in 292 to pagan parents. As a young adult, the kindness of Christians made a strong impression on him and he was converted and baptized in his early twenties. Inspired by the life of St. Antony of Egypt, Pachomius resolved to pursue the solitary life of a hermit. Legend says he heard a voice in his solitude instructing him to build a community for hermits. Thus, the first monastery was born.

He developed a corporate rule of life for the monastery that focused on love and sharing. Activities included daily prayers, rotating labor duties, religious instruction, recitation of Scripture, discussion of theology, meals, and sleep. One hundred monks lived at that first monastery, and Pachomius established at least six more over the course of his life. By the end of the fourth century, there were more than 7,000 monks involved in the movement he started.

TRY IT OUT

Memorize 1 Timothy 4:7-8: *"But have nothing to do with irreverent and silly myths. Rather, train yourself in godliness, for, the training of the body has a limited benefit, but godliness is beneficial in every way, since it holds promise for the present life and also for the life to come."*

Use the following table to begin writing your own rule of life. Think about incorporating the following as a start: prayer, community, Bible reading, journaling, Bible memorization, confession, retreat, service.

DAILY DISCIPLINES

WEEKLY DISCIPLINES

MONTHLY DISCIPLINES

ANNUAL DISCIPLINES

NOTES

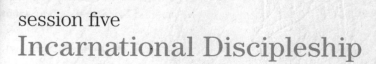

session five
Incarnational Discipleship

The landscape rolled by quickly outside the windows of her train car as it rambled down the tracks. The blurred images swept by; her life seemed to be doing the same. Had it really been more than 15 years since she first walked into that schoolroom?

Armed with knowledge and energized by passion, Agnes had been ready to give her new students everything she had. As she recalled the looks on their faces, a smile formed across hers. She was a white woman in a world of dark skin. Like all good teachers, her ears were attuned to even the slightest whispers, and she heard murmurings that she might be a devil or an evil spirit. Agnes had surveyed her classroom that first morning and had seen a mixture of fear, mischief, curiosity, and energy—a blend of attitudes ripe for learning. But she saw something else there, too—filth. How was she to teach Jesus to these children in such a place?

She dropped her carefully developed lesson plans on the desk and changed her plans for the first day of class. She rolled up her sleeves, found a bucket of water and a broom, and started cleaning the classroom. Slowly, the students joined the effort and in two hours, the classroom was completely transformed. But more importantly, the hearts of the children were transformed. She had won them.

When Agnes became the principal of the school, her mother sent her a letter, reminding her to care for the poor. The children of the school were poor. But the people she walked past every day endured an existence far worse than the children at the school. Hunger. Nakedness. Leprosy. The poverty and desperation were extreme. She loved her work at the school, but she could not shake the notion that there was something more she could do.

Several years later, Agnes received permission to begin a new mission to the poorest of the poor in Calcutta—the Missionaries of Charity. Today, we remember her as Mother Teresa.

TWENTY-FOUR HOURS IN NAIROBI

Two years have passed, and I'm still trying to wrap my head and heart around 24 life-altering hours of my life.

It began early in the morning as the group I was traveling with boarded a bus to head to the Sarova Panafric Hotel (the Waldorf-Astoria of Kenya) for a young professionals breakfast. I'll skip the part where I shot in projectile fashion the partially digested remains of my pre-breakfast of Pop-Tarts® near the carts of innocent and unsuspecting roadside merchants. At the breakfast, our group met lots of people just like us—attorneys, real estate agents, financial planners, and doctors. Our accents, it seemed, were the only things different about us. We served them through our encouragement, teaching, and prayers.

From there, we progressed directly to the Mathare slum, where only weeks before the Mungiki sect had beheaded political and tribal rivals. The poverty was extreme. The stench was unbearable. The sights were unbelievable. But we served: We played with the children. We prayed with the young mother infected with AIDS by a man who abdicated his family responsibilities. We laughed with the young orphan who had discovered the joy of God through the church located on the edge of the slum. We applauded the energetic performance of songs and Scripture recitations by the children of Baraka Christian Centre. We gave away picture books that told the story of Jesus in language the children could understand.

With no time to process either of the two experiences of the day, we grabbed a quick dinner and headed to the University of Nairobi, where we were scheduled to lead a small group leaders training for a campus ministry. Our meeting with the campus minister, Gibson, and his team remains a blur in my mind given the mentally and emotionally conflicted day. I tried my best to focus in on the next task—training and discipling the leaders of the next Kenyan generation. We shared ideas, encouraged them, prayed with them, and then enjoyed my favorite part of the day—sharing life with them around tables stocked with glass-bottled Coca-Colas®.

That night, it was impossible to wrap words around any of the three experiences or even process the inequity, disconnectedness, and disparateness between them. "Whiplash" was the word I wrote in my journal to describe the experience. We served in all three places, from the extravagance of the Panafric Hotel to the trash heaps of Mathare to the bright minds of Kenya's future.

It is estimated that 32.9 million people are living with HIV/AIDS. More than two-thirds, or 22 million, are living in Sub-Saharan Africa.

Listen to the audio segment called "Experimenting with Incarnational Discipleship" this week. Your group leader will send it to you via e-mail, or you can download it at *threadsmedia.com/sacredroads*. These audio recordings are designed to help you connect with different expressions of discipleship.

Here's where it got really confusing: I've always thought of serving as one person stooping down from his or her position to do something for someone else. The problem in these cases was that I had the haunting suspicion we weren't the ones serving, but the ones being served. But that's the unique blessing of service, isn't it? Incarnational ministry is both the result of our spiritual growth and the means to it.

INCARNATIONAL DISCIPLESHIP

The incarnational path of discipleship is physical, active, and tangible. It equates worship with activity. Like personal discipleship, it gained great popularity in the 19th and 20th centuries, but it focused on the outward instead of the inward. Within the framework of the incarnational model, people grew in their knowledge and relationship with Christ by seeking to become His hands and feet through service and outreach to others.

It's pretty easy to see the justification behind a discipleship philosophy built in this way. Discipleship, after all, is really the process of keeping in step with Jesus, becoming progressively more and more like Him and growing in intimacy of relationship with Him. If that's the goal, then it makes perfect sense that we would model our lives after the pattern of Jesus. Jesus is God incarnate. That is, He is God taking on humanity and coming to earth.

In a basic sense, the incarnation is God stooping low to get dirty amongst the dregs of humanity. If we want to truly follow Christ, which is really what being a disciple is all about, then we have to follow His pattern of living in this respect.

Kevin Blue said, "The kingdom of God is found in the dirty, grimy, common places of the world. And in his [God's] presence, we are all changed."[39] While personal discipleship would view outreach to others as a *result* of inward spiritual growth, incarnational discipleship would pursue outreach as a *means* of inward spiritual growth. Incarnational discipleship sees Jesus' call to action on behalf of the poor, sick, and oppressed as the channel by which we learn about Him, become more like Him, and grow in our relationship with Him.

While some wait expectantly for the kingdom of God to come, the incarnationalists seek to establish His kingdom in their own generation. They seek to become Jesus' hands and feet to the world around them and in the process, be transformed into His image.

One of the biggest proponents of incarnational discipleship is Shane Claiborne. Shane founded The Simple Way, a contemporary monastic movement described as "subversive friends conspiring to spread the vision of 'Loving God, loving people, and following Jesus,' in our neighborhoods and in our world." For more information, check out their Web site at *thesimpleway.org*.

What do you think is the relationship between inward development of holiness and outward expression of holiness?

Which should come first? Why?

The movie *Amazing Grace* tells the story of William Wilberforce, the Clapham Sect, and the abolishment of the slave trade. For books on the subject, check out *Amazing Grace in the Life of William Wilberforce* by John Piper and *Real Christianity* by William Wilberforce.

Several other groups emerged from the Clapham movement, including The Church Missionary Society (1799), The British and Foreign Bible Society (1804), and The Society for Bettering the Condition of the Poor (1796).

CLAPHAM, COMPASSION, AND CONTEXTUALIZATION

At the beginning of the second century, the church numbered about 50,000 people. While that's impressive growth considering the movement was started by a band of 12 Galileans, it was a very small group of people compared to the vast Roman world. But their impact was tangible and noticed by onlookers. Because early Christians had no opportunity to reform government programs, they decided to create their own. And in doing so, they offered a prophetic voice to the world. Government leaders took notice.

Aristides, a philosopher in Athens, described the work of Christians like this: "If anyone among them comes into want while they themselves have nothing to spare, they fast for two or three days for him. In this way they can supply any poor man with the food he needs."[40]

Emperor Julian echoed the way that Christians took care of one another and the outcasts of society around them: "Atheism (i.e. Christian faith) has been specially advanced through the loving service rendered to strangers, and through their care for the burial of the dead. It is a scandal that there is not a single Jew who is a beggar, and that the godless Galileans care not only for their own poor but for ours as well; while those who belong to us look in vain for the help that we should render them."[41]

While examples of incarnational discipleship have echoed throughout the past 2,000 years, it has certainly surged in application over the last two centuries. In 1790, the Clapham Sect, a modern model of Christian social concern, was born in England. Consisting of like-minded political leaders and social activists, the Clapham Sect was committed to the abolition of the slave trade.

William Wilberforce, a young member of Parliament and dedicated Christian, spearheaded the political effort. In 1807, a bill was passed to eradicate the slave trade. Shelley hails the Clapham success as "the shining example of how a society—perhaps the world itself—can be influenced by a few men of ability and devotion."[42]

Those efforts were the forerunners of two more contemporary movements that laid the foundation for incarnational discipleship—the social justice movement and the modern missions movement. Each of these contemporary incarnational movements came from a different theological stream.

The primary driving force behind the prominence of social justice awareness in churches today was the rise of the social gospel, pioneered by Washington Gladden (1836–1918) and Walter Rauschenbusch (1861–1918). A movement among liberal Protestant theologians and academics, it rightly sought to apply the gospel to ethics and social problems. Though flawed in its theology and application when taken to the extreme, the fundamental goal of the social gospel—to demonstrate the love of Jesus in practical ways—eventually penetrated all of the major denominations. Today, many major denominations have created leadership positions and departments to address social justice concerns, and most theological seminaries have expanded their curricula to include teaching on the Christian responsibility to these issues.

The 19th century also saw an explosion of evangelical mission to spread the spoken gospel around the world. An energetic young lay preacher named William Carey approached his leaders about forming a missionary society. Shockingly, one elderly man responded to his presentation, "Young man, sit down, sit down! You are an enthusiast. When God pleases to convert the heathen, He'll do it without consulting you or me."[43]

Carey, who would later earn the distinction as the "Father of Modern Missions," wrote "An Enquiry into the Obligations of Christians, to Use Means for the Conversion of the Heathens" in 1792. That same year, he formed the Baptist Missionary Society and headed to India. During the next 25 years, a dozen mission organizations were formed in America and Europe.

Carey and other missionaries recognized not only the value of language translation but also cultural contextualization of the gospel. Up until that point, becoming a Christian also largely meant

The life of John Newton significantly influenced the life of William Wilberforce and gave shape to the emergence of evangelicalism. A former slave ship captain who became an Anglican priest, Newton developed friendships with John Wesley, Charles Wesley, and George Whitefield. He shaped the spiritual growth and political worldview of Wilberforce, telling him that politics was as worthy a calling as that of a pastor. His song, "Amazing Grace," is his most famous legacy.

Dag Hammarskjöld was a Swedish diplomat who became the second secretary general of the United Nations in 1953. In September 1961, he died in a plane crash en route to negotiate a cease fire in the Congo. Nominated before his death, Hammarskjöld was granted the Nobel Peace Prize posthumously. He is quoted as saying, "The road to holiness necessarily passes through the world of action."[44]

embracing Western culture. A church might be started in the heart of Africa only to have Bibles in old English, sing English hymns, and dress in Western fashion.

Rather than promoting a conversion to Western culture, the missionaries of the 1800s began searching for ways to tell the gospel story in both the spoken language and the cultural language of the people they served. In 1865, Hudson Taylor adopted Chinese dress and customs as he took the message of Christ to the interior of China. Mary Slessor, a Scottish missionary, lived like an African as she worked tirelessly to rescue children, fight for the rights of women, reform the penal system, and spread the gospel in Nigeria. Recognizing the value of meeting personal needs, missionaries established schools, hospitals, and training centers for medical personnel. They improved health measures and taught more efficient and productive agricultural techniques.

Today, the activism of the Clapham Sect, the compassion of the social gospel, and the evangelistic fervor of the Protestant missionaries are found combined to various degrees in organizations such as the International Mission Board, Samaritan's Purse, The Simple Way, and WorldVision. Mission agencies continue to enlist people to translate the gospel in the languages and the cultures of people all over the world. Modern-day saints like the late Mother Teresa give their resources and their lives to the poor. And they all find that while they are serving, they are also growing. While they seek to share the gospel, they find that the gospel transforms them.

What is most important, inward transformation of your own life or outward transformation of the world around you? Why?

What risks do you see in leaning too far toward either issues of justice or the strictly spoken gospel?

How do you think you can effectively emphasize both?

In fairness to the members of the Pietist movement (which the incarnational movement largely rejected), they did express outwardly the changes they experienced inwardly. August Hermann Francke (1663–1727) began a school for the poor, started an orphanage, and established a hospital. Nikolaus von Zinzendorf worked with refugees.

INCARNATIONAL DISCIPLESHIP IN THE OLD TESTAMENT

The first cries for justice and compassion are heard most loudly in the prophets of the Old Testament. Whether crying foul at the misuse of power or pleading with people to turn from their sinfulness to God, there was a raw physicality to their ministry.

The shepherd Amos, whose name means "burden-bearer," dared to speak out during the prosperous but corrupt reign of Jeroboam II. The priest Amaziah, angered over the strong words of Amos, ordered him to cease and desist. But Amos continued to spread his message that righteousness and justice are essential to building healthy community and societies. He argued that religion is more than ceremony; it's right action and righteous living. Consider the following:

"Those who turn justice into wormwood throw righteousness to the ground" (Amos 5:7).

"I hate, I despise your feasts! I can't stand the stench of your solemn assemblies. Even if you offer Me your burnt offerings and grain offerings, I will not accept them; I will have no regard for your fellowship offerings of fattened cattle. Take away from Me the noise of your songs! I will not listen to the music of your harps. But let justice flow like water, and righteousness, like an unfailing stream" (Amos 5:21-24).

We hear similar warnings from the Book of Isaiah:

"Isn't the fast I choose: To break the chains of wickedness, to untie the ropes of the yoke, to set the oppressed free, and to tear off every yoke? Is it not to share your bread with the hungry, to bring the poor and homeless into your house, to clothe the naked when you see him, and to not ignore your own flesh and blood?" (Isaiah 58:6-7).

> **Do these passages in Amos and Isaiah change your understanding of God and His priorities? If so, how?**

> **Do these verses mean we should abandon fasting, giving, and worship and replace them with service? If not, how do these things work together?**

Amos, a shepherd, wrote one of the longer minor prophet books. He prophesied to Israel at the same time Hosea was prophesying to Israel, and while Micah and Isaiah were prophesying to Judah.

Amos didn't pull any punches in his prophecies. For example, check out Amos 4:1 (NLT), "Listen to me, you fat cows living in Samaria, you women who oppress the poor and crush the needy, and who are always calling to your husbands, 'Bring us another drink!'"

The Book of Isaiah is the first of the "major prophets," not because Isaiah was smarter, more spiritual, or more influential than other prophets, but because his book is longer than those labeled "minor prophets." He ministered during the reigns of kings Uzziah, Jotham, Ahaz, and Hezekiah. He lived under the threat of Assyria and witnessed Israel's fall to the Assyrians in 722 B.C. Isaiah means "Yahweh is salvation," and his book is sometimes called the "Old Testament Gospel."

Following in the footsteps of Jesus came Mother Teresa. Albanian by birth, Mother Teresa started a new order in Calcutta called The Missionaries of Charity, which she led for 45 years. At the time of her death, her movement was operating 610 missions in 123 countries, including hospices and homes for people with HIV/AIDS, leprosy, and tuberculosis; soup kitchens; children's and family counseling programs; orphanages; and schools.

The practice of foot washing was important in the dusty land of first-century Palestine, and it was usually performed by one of the more lowly servants. The practice continued in Christian circles and was mentioned by Tertullian, Augustine, and St. Benedict. It is celebrated in the Catholic Church as part of Holy Thursday. Some Baptists continue to observe the practice as a third ordinance, after baptism and Communion.

INCARNATIONAL DISCIPLESHIP IN THE LIFE OF CHRIST

"We are the only Jesus some people ever see." I used to think that meant that I'd better be really nice and always smiling. But the more I read about Jesus in the Gospels, the more radical I see that He is. And sadly, the more I grow in my relationship with Him, the more I realize how rarely I resemble Him. Think about it:

He bypassed the adults to hang out with the children. He skipped over the religious crowd to hang out with the homeless. He defied social conventions and touched the lepers. He cared for the sick, showed compassion for those who grieved, stopped to talk to beggars, sought out social outcasts, healed the lame, gave sight to the blind, and provided for basic needs. And He offended the religious leaders in the process.

His most clear challenge to service is found in Matthew 25:31-40, a parable about sheep and goats. According to His teaching, these two groups of people will be divided based on how they treated the hungry, thirsty, strangers, poor, sick, and imprisoned.

It's worth noticing that Jesus didn't say, "I was hungry and you donated funds to your local food bank," or "I was naked and you donated your old clothes to the Salvation Army." Obedience to Jesus' teaching requires much more of you than your money or resources. It requires personal investment of time, emotion, and touch. It's raw and tangible and physical.

> **List everything you have done in the past week that demonstrates obedience to Jesus' challenge in Matthew 25.**

> **What is one thing you can do next week to obey Jesus' challenge?**

His most clear challenge by example is found on the night before His crucifixion. On a night when Jesus could have understandably been concerned only about Himself, He picked up a towel and demonstrated in a powerful way what servant leadership really means.

Read John 13:1-5. What is most striking to you about this account?

I find this passage so interesting. First, it says, "He had loved his disciples during his ministry on earth, and now he loved them to the very end" (v. 1, NLT). Jesus' small group consisted of 12 losers. That's right—losers. Stinky Galilean fishermen, a traitor of a tax collector, and a wild-eyed anarchist zealot. But Jesus chose not to assume a position of top-down authority with these guys. Instead, He showed them the full extent of His love by serving them even in the midst of His own tragic circumstances.

Look at the next part: "Jesus knew that the Father had given him authority over everything . . . So he got up from the table, took off his robe, wrapped a towel around his waist, and poured water into a basin" (vv. 3-5). Jesus recognized His authority, and that recognition led Him not higher but lower, not to domination but to service.

> **When did you last demonstrate love? When was love last demonstrated to you?**

> **How do experiences like those help you grow in Christ?**

INCARNATIONAL DISCIPLESHIP IN THE NEW TESTAMENT

Service was central to the Christian community from the very beginning. Acts 2 and 4 record the radical acts of generosity of people selling their possessions to give to those who had need. Their acts weren't so much about redistribution of wealth as abundance of heart. That's made all the more clear in Acts 5 as Ananias and Sapphira were struck dead—not because they didn't give enough but because their hearts were dishonest in the process.

The first official positions of leadership created within the church were the deacons. Before pastors, bishops, or missionaries, a team of

Descending into Greatness by Bill Hybels is a call to servant leadership. He reminds his readers that Jesus is consistently pulling His followers down, asking them to follow Him to the least of these.

Madeleine L'Engle observed, "Half the world is starving; the other half is on a diet. We are not privileged because we deserve to be. Privilege accepted should mean responsibility accepted."

"Deacon" comes from the Greek word, *diakonos*, meaning a runner, servant, or messenger. *Diakonos* is found 30 times in the New Testament. Qualifications for a deacon are found in 1 Timothy 3:8-12.

Listen to "O Love That Will Not Let Me Go" by Sandra McCracken from the *Sacred Roads* playlist. Your group leader can e-mail you the whole playlist, or you can download it at *threadsmedia.com/sacredroads.*

seven men were appointed for the sake of serving. Today, the role of the deacon looks very different in many places. They pass the offering plate, make decisions about the church budget, and settle arguments about the color of the carpet. Those are all important responsibilities, but the heart of the deacon ministry is service to those in need and attendance to those whose voices may not be heard.

Paul instructed Christ-followers on the nature and priority of serving others. To him, freedom in Christ was vitally linked to service:

"For you are called to freedom, brothers; only don't use this freedom as an opportunity for the flesh, but serve one another through love. For the entire law is fulfilled in one statement: You shall love your neighbor as yourself" (Galatians 5:13-14).

This is an echo of the Old Testament prophets who cried for mercy over sacrifice and service over celebration. James, too, wrote at length about the interconnectedness of faith and outward expressions of it. It's a chicken and egg situation—what comes first, faith or works? On one hand, our works are an expression of our faith. At the same time, our faith is built by our works.

Read James 2:14-26. What is the relationship between faith and works? Which comes first?

Consider Galatians 5:13-14. What is the relationship between freedom and service?

PUTTING IT INTO PRACTICE

Missions, service, outreach, and hospitality are all interconnected and parts of each other. However, for the sake of consideration and discussion, let's look at each individually.

MISSIONS

For the purposes of this study, we will talk about missions in the sense of cross-cultural communication of the gospel—in both word and action. In today's world, that can happen on the other side of your cubicle, down the hall of your dorm, or across the ocean.

Jesus left His disciples with an impossible mission: "Go, therefore, and make disciples of all nations" (Matthew 28:19). Acts 1:8 breaks it down more strategically:

"But you will receive power when the Holy Spirit has come upon you, and you will be My witnesses in Jerusalem, in all Judea and Samaria, and to the ends of the earth."

God's heart for the world is seen all the way back in the Book of Genesis, when God promised Abraham that all the nations of the world would be blessed through him. This promise roots missions in what God—not we—will do. We are privileged to participate in His work; it's not an obligation we're expected to accomplish ourselves. God's vision is progressing through history and will culminate on the day when representatives from every tribe and language and people and nation will stand redeemed by the blood of Jesus.

You can be involved in missions by giving, praying, and going. Matthew 6:21 says, "For where your treasure is, there your heart will be also." It's quite possible that your budget is the greatest reflection of your spiritual maturity, and changes to your budget may have the greatest potential for spiritual growth. If discipleship is about growing to be more like Jesus, and where you invest your finances reveals and redirects the focus of your life, then giving to advance the gospel throughout the world might be the most spiritual thing you can do.

Missions also requires an investment of prayer. Missionaries and their families covet prayer for their safety, the health of their children, finances, and the success of their ministry. Prayer is also needed for the millions of people who have never heard the gospel in their own language or who do not have a sustainable church in their culture. Talk to your pastor about areas of the world where your church is involved in missions and the missionaries you support.

Finally, missions involves going. Short-term mission trips have been the focus of ultimate praise and utter disdain. Imagine a team of 12 teenagers who raise $3,000 each to minister in the poverty-stricken slums of India. Now imagine the teenagers just sending the money they raised to the poor rather than going themselves. Many argue that the latter option is a much more efficient and reasonable use of those resources—no flight costs, no time invested in developing skits, no sick teenagers, no mid-mission pep talks to a bunch of kids who are missing their iPods—just resources invested directly into the lives of the people who need them the most.

The Joshua Project is a ministry of the U.S. Center for World Mission which focuses on evangelism and missions to unreached people groups. It estimates that 2.74 billion individuals live in approximately 6,631 unreached people groups in the 10/40 Window, the area of the world least affected by the gospel. Learn more about unreached people groups, prayer needs, and how you can get involved at *joshuaproject.net*.

The 10/40 Window is the rectangular area of North Africa, the Middle East, and Asia between 10 degrees north and 40 degrees north latitude. The vast majority of the world's unreached people groups live in that region.

To learn more about missions, consider taking the Perspectives course offered by the U. S. Center for World Mission (*uscwm.org*).

But that evaluation fails to take into account the life-changing potential of lives intersecting with lives. I've witnessed the intangibles of short-term missions work—people who are blessed beyond belief that teenagers from the United States would spend their hard-earned money and "waste" their spring break just to come to their country and connect with them. I've seen the missionaries and the pastors who are blessed that people back home are praying for them and taking their message back. That's not to mention the dramatic life change a mission experience has on the one who goes. Their world becomes suddenly bigger, and they are more passionate about issues and cultures needing the gospel than ever before.

Right or wrong, it seems that short-term missionaries are blessed way beyond the level of blessing they bestow because they are experiencing incarnational discipleship. Hopefully, that experience transforms them, ultimately resulting in more giving, more praying, and more going.

Do you agree or disagree with the argument that short-term mission trips are a good investment of resources? Why?

How can you be involved with missions in your own city? How about around the world?

You can find prayer updates, pressing global needs, and opportunities for service online at *imb.org* (International Mission Board) and *namb.net* (North American Mission Board).

Here are some practical ways you can involve yourself or your Bible study group in missions:

- Go on a mission trip. Check with your church or denomination to see if there are upcoming trips you can participate in. Or, look at a mission organization like the North American Mission Board, the International Mission Board, or the Navigators.
- Adopt a missionary. Commit to pray for them, correspond with them, and send them support when possible.
- Pray for a specific country or people group.
- Pack a shoebox for Samaritan's Purse's Operation Christmas Child.
- Contact the local office of a mission organization such as WorldVision or Compassion to see how you or your group can get involved.

SERVICE

It's impossible to separate service and missions, but for the sake of clarity, we'll define service as sharing the love of Jesus through action in the communities in which we live. At NCC, we have a core value: Love people when they least expect it and least deserve it. That's what service is all about.

In John 9, Jesus and the disciples encountered a man who was born blind. Instead of simply touching him or declaring him to be healed, Jesus did something different. Check it out:

"After He said these things He spit on the ground, made some mud from the saliva, and spread the mud on his eyes. 'Go,' He told him, 'wash in the pool of Siloam' (which means "Sent"). So he left, washed, and came back seeing" (John 9:6-7).

Now, there are a lot of theories about why Jesus did this, but I don't find those theories nearly as fascinating as another question: How many times did Jesus have to spit in that dirt to make enough mud to smear over the man's eyes? Imagine the scene. Dry, dusty Palestine. The Son of God, hovered over, spitting repeatedly on the ground while onlookers watched. Every now and then, bringing healing to another means getting down in the middle of the mess of their lives. And hacking up some loogies. Ministry is messy, but it forms the character of Christ within us.

Too often we view service as a "project" instead of a lifestyle. It's easier to participate in a project once a year that makes us feel good than to make the hard lifestyle choices that bring true change. Nevertheless, projects are good starting points and foundational to the environments in which lives begin to be transformed.

> **How can you move from viewing service with a project mentality to a lifestyle mentality?**

> **Write down five ways you think you could participate in service in your community.**

If you haven't already read them, grab a copy of *Interrupted* by Jen Hatmaker and *Red Revolution* by Adam Thomason. They will help you discover more about God's heart for the world and the role He has created for you and called you to play.

"Grace is love that cares and stoops and rescues."
—John Stott

Here are some ideas about how to experiment with service:

- Do something in your community—clean up a bus stop, pick up the trash, take cookies to your neighbors, offer free car washes.
- Fast a meal and give the money to someone in need.
- Make sandwiches and take them to the homeless.
- Volunteer at a shelter or a soup kitchen.

HOSPITALITY

In the book *Radical Hospitality*, authors Daniel Homan and Lonni Collins Pratt explain, "Hospitality has two meanings for most people today. It either refers to hotels or cruise ships, or it is connected to entertaining friends and family in the warmth of candlelight with gleaming silver and ivory lace. One model makes it an industry, thereby assigning some productive use to it and making it profitable. The other model relegates it to the domain of entertainment and housekeeping, generally considered women's work. Thus, it has become safe and cozy, even productive, rather than revolutionary, risky, and world-rattling."[48]

When I think of hospitality, I often think of teacups and doilies and good manners and well-set tables. That is all well and good and certainly a dimension of hospitality. But the more I delve into the biblical examples, the more I'm realizing that hospitality is much more. It's about inviting people into your life, sharing your everyday and intimate experiences. It's about embracing uncertainty and risk and welcoming the stranger in the hopes of bringing the power, presence, protection, and provision of God to their lives as well as ours.

At its core, hospitality is about inviting someone into your life and sharing your life with them. When you look at hospitality offered and accepted throughout the Bible, sometimes the blessings of God were bestowed on the giver and other times they were bestowed on the receiver. In most cases, though, the blessing was poured out on both.

When was the last time you experienced genuine hospitality? How did it make you feel?

Read each of the following passages:
- Genesis 18:1-15
- Joshua 2:1-21
- 1 Kings 17:8-24
- 2 Kings 4:9-37
- Luke 10:30-37
- Acts 9:10-19

R

In *Refrigerator Rights*, Drs. Will Miller and Glenn Sparks talk about the true test of community— whether or not an individual has the permission to open your refrigerator, pull out ingredients, and make himself a sandwich. Pick up a copy to learn more about hospitality and community.

To motivate you in the area of incarnational discipleship, watch the video called "Something's Missing" during your small group discussion. This video will engage the idea that you grow while serving others. You can also download the video for yourself at *threadsmedia.com/sacredroads*.

What do you learn about hospitality from each? In each passage, who receives the greater blessing—the receiver of the hospitality or the one who gives it?

Here are some ways to experiment with the practice of hospitality:

- Cook dinner for a family or some college students who might appreciate a home-cooked meal.
- Befriend an international student.
- Have a visiting missionary stay in your home.
- Accept the hospitality of someone else.

ACTIVISM

John Hasler is my friend and co-conspirator in the discipleship department of NCC. John is always protesting something. War. Big business. My blog posts. During a recent season of political activity, he was shocked by the lack of planned protests and I was certain he would launch his own protest against laziness and complacency. While I can't say I agree with everything he chooses to take a stand for or against (in fact he sometimes makes me crazy), I admire his guts to step out and speak up, and I'm consistently challenged to put feet to faith in a very practical way.

But John doesn't just protest. He also creates. He reinvigorated a ministry to the homeless, growing it from a committed few making 10 lunches a week to an army of volunteers distributing around 100 lunches every Sunday. He started a Bible Study and dinner on Wednesday nights that created community for people who lived in traditional homes, but also for those living in shelters and on the streets. He spearheaded our annual Week of Justice, which educates and motivates action on issues such as poverty, modern-day slavery, and unfair trade and labor practices. Most people know John because of what he's for more than because of what he's against.

Michelangelo said, "Criticize by creating."[49] While protest has a place in the history of Christian activism, bringing real change requires more than speaking out against something. Like William Wilberforce, Mother Teresa, and John Hasler, you must create.

Here's a list of other organizations you might check out to broaden your experience with incarnational discipleship:

Samaritan's Purse
(*samaritanspurse.org*)

Blood Water Mission
(*bloodwatermission.com*)

Compassion International
(*compassion.com*)

Baptist Global Response
(*baptistglobalresponse.com*)

Operation World
(*operationworld.org*)

Feeling a little overwhelmed about changing the world as you grow in Christ? Pick up a copy of *Practical Justice* by Kevin Blue for some everyday suggestions about how you can make a difference.

The first step is being informed. If you want to make a difference in the world around you, you must be able to be relevant to the culture. Both biblical exegesis and cultural exegesis are required. Secondly, pray. And read the newspaper through the lens of Scripture. Ask God to reveal to you His heart on the situation.

Finally, do something. Speak up. Write a letter. Protest. March. Love. Let your actions shout louder than your words. For 2,000 years, Christians have lifted their voices for those who have no voice and made a difference in a variety of social arenas—slavery, abortion, prison reform, human trafficking, education, and so on.

When thinking about what social issues you should participate in, it's helpful to think in terms of what makes you happy, what makes you cry, and what makes you angry. What social issues do those things to you?

Is it better for a Christian to try to change the laws or to change the culture? Why?

How does activism in particular contribute to the process of discipleship?

Here are some ideas for getting involved:

- Adopt a cause—choose by thinking about what makes you pound your fist on the table.
- Pick a topic and learn more about it—sweatshop labor, abortion, trade, human trafficking, slavery, and racism are just a few to get you thinking.
- Watch a documentary highlighting one of these issues.
- Host a "Justice Night" at your church to educate, inspire, and motivate.
- Write a letter to a political official who has the ability to influence the issue that concerns you.

The documentary *As We Forgive* by Laura Waters Hinson highlights what is possible when Christians dare to believe that Jesus can be the solution. Attempting the impossible, they are bringing hope to victims of the 1994 Rwandan genocide and facilitating forgiveness between perpetrators and victims. Watch the trailer and learn more at *asweforgivemovie.com*.

Lottie Moon is probably the best known of all Southern Baptist missionaries. She spent nearly 40 years in China as a teacher and evangelist, promoting the call for women to have an equal role in mission efforts at a time when most missionaries were married men. She also promoted the idea of contextualizing the gospel, dressing in Chinese clothes and adopting Chinese customs. She eventually died of malnutrition due to her constant willingness to share her personal finances and food with those around her.

DARE TO EXPLORE

The most spiritual thing you can do for yourself might be something that you do for someone else. I've discovered that spiritual slumps are often overcome by serving others. And while I value personal discipleship and relational discipleship, I think even those modes are enhanced and improved when practiced in conjunction with service to others.

There are dangers, however; the first being that you may miss the point entirely. Service without the message of the cross is merely humanitarian aid. There's certainly nothing wrong with that, but it's not the gospel and not what the church is about. Be careful that your action doesn't become separated from a Christian worldview. A related danger is that you become so busy helping others that you neglect your own spiritual growth. Leaning into personal discipleship along with serving others will help offset this.

We must also be careful that we don't become more political than Christian. Despite our differences or what side of the Congressional aisle we might land, we are first and foremost members of the body of Christ, and Jesus should be our first allegiance. Some people become frustrated because the church—either their local body or the church as a whole—isn't moving fast enough on an issue that is important to them, so they separate themselves from the church. But instead of being frustrated, become part of the solution. Celebrate the positive (though small) steps and keep encouraging people to care about the things God cares about.

There's also one other potential problem emerging—trendiness. Can I say that? It's trendy to care about poor people right now. Hollywood is doing it. Christian celebrities are doing it. If you want to be a "cool" Christian today, it seems you need to care about certain social and political issues. Make sure that you are pursuing incarnational discipleship because you want to become more like Jesus, not to manipulate your own reputation.

What other problems and pitfalls might be related to incarnational discipleship if taken too far or pursued to the exclusion of other methods?

Mother Teresa, who spent 45 years ministering to the poor, orphaned, and sick of India, acknowledged that not every person is called to devote their lives to the poor. She did say, however, that "God does call everyone to a Calcutta; you have to find yours."

ANOTHER VOICE—ANOTHER ERA
ST. FRANCIS OF ASSISI (C. 1182–1226)

St. Francis of Assisi, whose given birth name was Giovanni, was the son of a wealthy merchant. The first biography of his life describes his youth, "Up to the twenty-fifth year of his age, he squandered and wasted his time miserably."[51] He desired to become a decorated knight, but he was captured in battle and imprisoned for a year. After returning to Assisi, he went through a period of reflection and repentance that proved to be a significant turning point in his life.

Choosing the life of a hermit, he lived in an abandoned church and began to distribute his father's wealth to the poor. Enraged, Francis' father dragged him before the local bishop, demanding that justice be served and his money be returned. Francis responded by stripping off his clothing, renouncing his heritage, and proclaiming that God was his only Father.

For the remainder of his life, he lived among the sick, the poor, and the outcasts. During the Crusades, he daringly crossed enemy lines to share the gospel with the Muslims. He even spent a month with the Sultan, trying to persuade him to become a Christian. Soon Francis gathered a group of followers, and started the order "Friars Minor" or "Little Brothers." The church canonized him as a saint within two years of his death.

TRY IT OUT

Memorize Matthew 25:40: *"And the King will answer them, 'I assure you: Whatever you did for one of the least of these brothers of Mine, you did for Me.'"*

For the next week, employ the advice of Karl Barth, holding the Bible in one hand and the newspaper in the other. Watch the nightly news with a prayer journal. As the stories are reported, note specific ways to pray for people across your community and the world.

NOTES

conclusion
Discipleship Next

So what's next? What will discipleship look like in the future? Hopefully, it will look more balanced. Throughout history, discipleship has tended to emphasize one particular road of following Jesus. Maybe the future of discipleship looks like the integration of all the historic sacred roads into a well-rounded pursuit of Christ-likeness.

But those roads will look different than they have in the past. We've got to re-engineer and re-imagine discipleship for our generation and make our contribution to the grand story God is writing throughout history.

Like the preceding chapters, it seems that the sacred roads of discipleship in our generation will twist and turn with the prevailing philosophies and emerging technologies of the day. And in our day, mobility and technology have radically changed the way we learn and relate to one another. Drs. Will Miller and Glenn Sparks' book *Refrigerator Rights* explores these themes. Consider some of their findings:

- According to the 2000 census, more than 16 percent of the population moved their residence during the census period.
- One third of young adults ages 20-29 moved in one year— from 1999 to 2000.
- Nearly 45 million Americans move every year, and the average American moves every five to six years, thereby rupturing significant relationships with family and friends.

The technological surge of the past 50 years has also impacted our connection points.

- Roughly one-fourth of America's dinners are eaten while watching television.
- Nearly 60 percent of children watch at least two hours of television a day.[52]

How do these statistics compare with your personal involvement with mobility and technology?

How do you think these trends are affecting the way we should approach discipleship?

Some would argue that these statistics reveal a sickness in society, and the church should be a prophetic voice of sanity and clarity by living counter-culturally. Maybe I'm young and naïve, but I'm more interested in embracing the reality and doing the hard of work of building community and making disciples in the midst of the chaos. So let's consider some of the characteristics of the 21st century and imagine what sacred road of discipleship we might find weaving through it.

Do you think it's possible that there are ways of doing church and discipling people that no one has thought of before? Why or why not?

WORLDWIDE WEB

The body of Christ has always been a worldwide web of people from varying cultures, languages, and geographies, but we can see it more clearly now than ever before as technology has shrunk our world. Relationships are no longer bound by geography, and the body of Christ seems to grow bigger and smaller all at the same time. We are moving more frequently, but we are staying connected as closely to those an ocean away as we are to those who work in the cubicle next to us. Because relationships are changing, relational discipleship is changing. So how do you practice relational discipleship in a world where people rarely stay in one place for more than a few years?

There are definitely challenges. Cultivating authentic and transparent community often requires years of trust-building and experience sharing. But what about the advantages? We have the ability to touch hundreds of lives that eventually go to all corners of the globe. In the end, mobility means doing discipleship on the go.

"Discipleship on the go" doesn't really work in a program-oriented setting. Fortunately, "programs" weren't the discipleship approach of Jesus, either. He didn't take His disciples through a training program; He trained these followers on the road, on the sea, at parties, and at wells. Discipleship happened on the move, and it revolved around the experiences they were having. Three years later, those men changed history. Instead of viewing discipleship as a program, our mobility is forcing us to approach every situation and conversation as an opportunity for discipleship. We do that by being intentional in the people we associate with and taking advantage of every opportunity we have with someone because we might not ever have another.

Relational discipleship today is also happening online. LifeChurch.tv was one of the first churches to launch online small groups. Innovations like these stem from the church's core value: "to reach people that no one is reaching you have to do things that no one is doing."[53] Online small groups are advantageous in that you can be in a group with friends across the country, you can attend in your bathrobe if you're sick, you don't have to coordinate snack schedules, and they are convenient and non-threatening to those who are new to groups. Today, LifeChurch.tv hosts dozens of online small groups, with studies ranging from Bible study to marriage preparation to prison ministry.

What are some practical ways you can do discipleship on the go or online?

It has been argued that the prevalence of social network has actually increased levels of isolation and withdrawal. Do the advantages of using social networking for discipleship outweigh the disadvantages? Why or why not?

What are some other potential pitfalls or problems that might be associated with relational discipleship in our generation?

HIGH DEFINITION

The emergence of new technologies means that we can take experiential discipleship to a new level. In general, all of our experiences are bigger, louder, and more stimulating because of modern technology.

The annual Catalyst Conference in Atlanta blends leadership development and spiritual challenge with the latest in audio-visual technology. Like the medieval Mass, participants are immersed in an environment where they are saturated by images, sounds, and other sensory stimuli that deliver not only a feeling, but also convey truth through experience.

At NCC, we've embraced media and technology to make disciples. At a recent Good Friday service, we experimented with a lectio divina/Stations of the Cross experience that combined epic soundtracks, worship music, visual art, and Scripture readings. We used the movie screens like the medieval church used stained glass—to tell the stories of faith (in this case, the Passion narrative) in pictures. We have expanded our weekend worship experiences to five locations through high definition video. We record the weekend message at our live service on Saturday nights and download the video on hard drives that are distributed to our video locations on Sunday morning.

Beyond the video message, technology is also enabling church to happen online. As of the writing of this book, I know of at least 30 churches have Internet campuses that allow members to experience church online. (As I was writing this section, I wasn't sure how many churches had Internet campuses so I posted a question on Twitter. Two connections and 30 minutes later, I had my answer.)

What are some technologically-aided worship experiences you've been part of?

Are there potential problems and pitfalls that might be associated with experiential discipleship in our generation?

WORD OF MOUSE

Technology has also changed the way we experience intellectual discipleship. For 2,000 years, the gospel has spread by word of mouth. Now we have added the opportunity to spread the gospel by word of mouse. The Internet provides access to more Bible study resources and theological training in minutes than Martin Luther had over the course of his entire life.

Just consider these two helpful sites: *biblegateway.com* and *youversion.com*. Biblegateway allows users to reach and search in 20 different English translations. If you prefer to read in Spanish, Icelandic, or Haitian Creole, it offers those options as well. Reading plans, commentaries, and Bible dictionaries can also be accessed on the site. The YouVersion of the Bible is one of the most exciting developments for intellectual discipleship. It contains the Bible in 40 versions and 22 languages and allows you to read different versions in parallel. You can create Bible reading plans, comment on the text, and interact with other people who are reading the same Scriptures. YouVersion works on the go, offering free apps for your mobile phone, iPhone, or BlackBerry.

Many churches are moving to Web-based video and resources to train small group leaders. Seacoast Church in South Carolina offers new leader training using on-demand video training within their "My Next Steps" corner of their Web site (*mynextsteps.org*). Threads, the publisher of this Bible study, has a host of leader articles, video, and statistics designed to influence leaders in churches (*threadsmedia. com*). Small Group Exchange (*smallgroupexchange.com*) provides free online training from some of the best small group pastors and communicators of our day to train all levels of teachers and leaders in the church.

Technology is opening new opportunities for the biblical and theological training of pastors at home and abroad. In fact, I'm writing this conclusion from the online campus of Regent University, where my husband Ryan is currently pursuing a divinity degree online.

One problem we face with online intellectual discipleship is that the Internet is filled with self-proclaimed prophets and theologians. What are some good practices for discerning the good and the bad?

What are some other potential problems and pitfalls that might be associated with intellectual discipleship in our generation?

CONFESSIONALS AND LIBRARIES TO GO

Though it may seem counterintuitive, modernity and technology have facilitated new expressions of the rhythms of personal discipleship. Spiritual disciplines like journaling, silence, solitude, and confession are both necessitated by and enhanced by the prevalence of technology in our culture.

Matt Chandler, lead pastor of the Village Church in Texas, is working to implement a Web-based survey that would assess spiritual growth and areas for improvement in the lives of the church's members. The program would include a self-assessment of beliefs and practices that gives members guidance on how to chart a course for personal discipleship. The results would include suggestions for small group opportunities, equipping classes, and conferences in the area that could be recommended as potential next steps.[54]

Other churches have experimented with online confessionals. Sites such as *mysecret.tv* and *ivescrewedup.com* allow people to anonymously make confessions and receive feedback from other site users. *Mysecret.tv* admits that it's not the ultimate solution, but a step in the right direction: "It's not an end-all, be-all solution, but a place to begin the process and find the hope that can be found in acknowledging that carrying the burden of your shame alone will get you nowhere."[55]

For me, blogging has become a form of spiritual journaling. My blog serves as a diary of daily activities, a repository of Bible study notes, a list of prayer requests, a log of written prayers, and a notebook of lessons that God is teaching me. While I still find great value in journaling with a piece of paper and a pen, I've found that there is a level of accountability built into the blog platform, and it serves a double purpose of facilitating another avenue of relational discipleship.

Previous generations had to go to great lengths to procure resources to help them in their pursuits of personal discipleship. It required a trip out to the desert mystics to listen and observe their spiritual disciplines or a trip to a local monastery to look at the books in their library. If you were very wealthy, you could commission the creation of private prayer books, devotional books, and hymnals.

Today, it's much more convenient to gather resources that facilitate personal discipleship, and it only takes a quick trip to the modern monastic library—the strip mall bookstore or the click of a mouse on *Amazon.com*. Amazon's Kindle device has made our personal libraries portable. Kindle contains about 1.4GB of space, which is enough to carry approximately 1,500 books.

James 5:16 states that we find healing when we confess to one another. Can this be facilitated in an online environment? Why or why not?

What are some other potential problems and pitfalls that might be associated with personal discipleship in our generation?

VIRTUAL MISSIONS

Our affinity for mobility and technology has spurred our involvement in incarnational discipleship in ways that previous generations could not have imagined. Most importantly, our quick access to world news and connections across the globe has raised our level of awareness concerning the needs around the world. Heading to the mission field today costs us a plane ticket and a week's vacation (instead of a boat ride for months), and we pack our clothes in a suitcase (instead of a coffin). So thousands

more are able to participate in these kinds of spiritual growth experiences.

The gospel is even being spread through online mission trips. At NCC, we set a goal of sending 10 percent of NCCers on mission and we planned 10 mission trip options. Our digital pastor, David Russell, suggested that we consider launching an online mission trip. None of us knew exactly what that meant, but we found it intriguing.

My friend Alan Danielson from Journey Church in Oklahoma recently led his small group (which meets in an online forum) on an online mission trip. The group met together online for a few minutes to pray together and strategize. Then, they left to enter their own worlds of Facebook, Twitter, and other social networking sites.

Each group member updated their Facebook and Twitter statuses with the following post: "For the next 20-30 minutes I'm going to be praying with and for friends online. If you want me to pray for something specific please let me know." Then, they reached out to friends and family who don't have relationships with Christ, asking them if there was any way in which they could pray for them. After the 30-minute online mission experiment, the group came back together to discuss what they had experienced.[56]

Mobility and technology have made mission experiences and service more convenient. Is that convenience ultimately a positive or negative development? Why?

What are some other potential problems and pitfalls that might be associated with incarnational discipleship in our generation?

DARE TO EXPLORE

A Christian prisoner in Cuba was once asked to sign a statement containing charges against fellow Christians that would lead to their arrest. He said, "The chain keeps me from signing this." The officer protested, "But you are not in chains!" "I am," said the Christian. "I am bound by the chain of witnesses who throughout the centuries gave their lives for Jesus Christ. I am a link in this chain. I will not break it."[57]

In 2 Timothy 2:2, Paul passed the baton of leadership to Timothy and ultimately to the faithful men who Timothy would teach. We live in that chain, and we must do our part to expand the kingdom of God in our generation. We must strive to become more like Christ, and we must invest our time and resources into helping others become more like Him. I believe we are living at the most exciting and hopeful time in the history of the church. Like every generation, we have been dealt our share of philosophical quagmires and cultural challenges. We can view them as pitfalls and problems, or we can view them as the greatest opportunities the church has ever seen.

We have received a rich legacy from those who dared to follow the red letter challenges of Jesus over the last 2,000 years. Let's walk along the sacred roads laid by those who have come before us and explore the historic paths of discipleship. And let's make our own contribution. Let's explore the sacred roads that have been left to us, learn the craft of sacred road building, and cut roads into new territory that can be explored by the generations that follow us.

END NOTES

INTRODUCTION
1. Bruce Shelley, *Church History in Plain Language* (Nashville: Thomas Nelson Publishers, 1995), *xv*.

SESSION 1
2. Julie Gorman, *Community That Is Christian* (Grand Rapids, MI: Baker Books, 2002), 229.
3. Henri Nouwen, *Out of Solitude* (Notre Dame: Ave Marie Press, 2004), 38.
4. Gerald Sittser, *Water from a Deep Well* (Downers Grove, IL: Intervarsity Press, 2007), 59, 62.
5. Peter Brown, as quoted in *Deep Well*, Sittser, 62.
6. Justin Martyr, as quoted in *History of the Christian Church* [CD-ROM] by Philip Schaff, Copyright © 1999, 2003 by Biblesoft, Inc.
7. Stanley Grenz, *Theology for the Community of God* (Grand Rapids, MI: Wm. B. Eerdmans Publishing Co., 2000), 179.
8. Justin Martyr, as quoted in *Deep Well*, Sittser, 60.
9. Gorman, *Community*, 94.
10. C. S. Lewis, *The Four Loves* (Orlando, FL: Harcourt Publishing, 1991), 2.
11. Edgar Guest, as quoted in *The Lost Art of Disciple Making*, Leroy Eims (Grand Rapids, MI: Zondervan, 1978), 102.

SESSION 2
12. Shelley, *Church History*, 184.
13. Robert Webber, *Ancient-Future Faith* (Grand Rapids, MI: Baker Academic, 1999), 97.
14. *Ibid.*
15. Henri Nouwen, *The Return of the Prodigal Son* (NY: Doubleday Publishing Group, 1994), 107.
16. *Holman Illustrated Bible Dictionary* (Nashville: Holman Bible Publishers, 2003), 1052.
17. Patrick Kavanaugh, "J. S. Bach: For the Glory of God," *Christianity Today* [online], 1 July 2005 [cited 11 March 2009]. Available from the Internet: *http://ctlibrary.com*
18. Paul S. Minear, "Bach and Today's Theologians," *Theology Today* [online], [cited 11 March 2009]. Available from the Internet: *http://theologytoday.ptsem.edu*

SESSION 3
19. Mark Buchanan, *The Rest of God* (Nashville: Thomas Nelson, 2007), 4.
20. Martin Luther, as quoted in *Deep Well*, Sittser, 217.
21. Shelley, *Church History*, 243.
22. *Ibid.*, 312.
23. Dallas Willard, *The Great Omission: Reclaiming Jesus's Essential Teachings on Discipleship* (San Fanscisco: HarperSanFrancisco, 2006), 180.
24. A.W. Tozer, *The Knowledge of the Holy* (New York: Harper and Row, 1961), 10.
25. D. L. Moody, as quoted in *Bible Study Methods: Twelve Ways You Can Unlock God's Word*, Rick Warren (Grand Rapids, MI: Zondervan, 2006), 16.
26. Stanley Grenz, *Who Needs Theology?* (Downers Grove, IL: InterVarsity Press, 1996), 14.
27. *http://www.giga-usa.com/quotes/topics/study_t001.htm*
28. Dallas Willard, *Renovation of the Heart* (Colorado Springs, CO: NavPress, 2002), 95.

SESSION 4
29. Shelley, *Church History*, 432.
30. Eusebius as quoted in *Streams of Living Water*, Richard Foster (New York: Harper Collins, 1998), 69.
31. Martin Luther as quoted in *Celebration of Discipline,* Richard Foster (New York: Harper Collins, 1998), 34.
32. John Ortberg, *The Life You've Always Wanted* (Grand Rapids, MI: Zondervan, 2002), 77.
33. Dave Buehring, *A Discipleship Journey* (Franklin, TN: OceanHill Communications, 2004), 109.

34. Thomas à Kempis, *The Imitation of Christ* (North Brunswick, NJ: Bridge-Logos Publishers, 1999), 48.
35. *http://www.quotationspage.com/quote/29375.html*
36. Ortberg, *Life*,188.
37. Richard Foster, *Celebration of Discipline* (San Francisco: HarperSanFrancisco, 1988), 20.
38. à Kempis, *Imitation*, 48.

SESSION 5
39. Kevin Blue, *Practical Justice* (Downers Grove, IL: InterVarsity Press, 2006), 18.
40. Aristides as quoted in *Deep Well*, Sittser, 54.
41. Emperor Julian as quoted in *Church History*, Shelley, 35-36.
42. Ibid., 369.
43. William Carey as quoted in *Deep Well*, Sittser, 274.
44. *http://www.dictionary-quotes.com/in-our-era-the-road-to-holiness-necessarily-passes-through-the-world-of-action-dag-hammarskjold/*
45. Madeline L'Engle as quoted in *The Westminster Collection of Christian Quotations* by Martin H. Manser (Louisville, KY: Westminster John Knox Press, 2001), 318.
46. *http://www.joshuaproject.net/great-commission-statistics.php*
47. *http://www.tentmaker.org/Quotes/grace_quotes.html*
48. Lonni Collins Pratt and Daniel Homan, *Radical Hospitality: Benedict's Way of Love* (Brewster, MA: Paraclete Press, 2002), 10.
49. *http://en.wikiquote.org/wiki/Michelangelo*
50. Mary Poplin, "Finding Our Own Calcutta: Mother Teresa and the Infinite God Dying of Love," *The Other Journal* [online], 4 February, 2009 [cited 26 March, 2009]. Available from the Internet: *www.theotherjournal.com*
51. St. Francis of Assisi as quoted in *Streams of Living Water*, Richard Foster, 99.

CONCLUSION
52. Will Miller and Glenn Sparks, *Refrigerator Rights* (New York: Berkley Publishing Group, 2002), 48,63,85.
53. Craig Groeschel, "To reach people that no one is reaching you have to do things that no one is doing" (video), *Church Crunch* [online], 17 April 2009 [cited 1 June 2009]. Available from the Internet: *http://churchcrunch.com*
54. Matt Chandler, "Where Do We Go From Here?" sermon manuscript, [online], delivered 21 February 2009 [cited 22 May 2009]. Available from the Internet: *http://hv.thevillagechurch.net/sermons*
55. *Mysecret.tv* [online], [cited 1 June 2009]. Available from the Internet: *http://mysecret.tv/about.php*
56. Alan Danielson, "Online Group Mission," *AlanDanielson.TV* [online], 28 May 2009 [cited 1 June 2009]. Available from the Internet: *http://alandanielson.spruz.com*
57. DC Talk and the Voice of the Martyrs, *Jesus Freaks* (Tulsa, OK: Albury Publishers, 1999), 49.

WHAT IS THREADS?

WE ARE A COMMUNITY OF YOUNG ADULTS—
people who are piecing the Christian life together, one experience at a time. Threads is driven by four key markers that are essential to young adults everywhere, and though it's always dangerous to categorize people, we think these are helpful in reminding us why we do what we do.

First of all, we are committed to being responsible. That is, doing the right thing. Though we're trying to grow in our understanding of what that is, we're glad we already know what to do when it comes to recycling, loving our neighbor, tithing, or giving of our time.

Community is also important to us. We believe we all need people. People we call when the tire's flat and people we call when we get the promotion. And it's those people—the day-in-day-out people—that we want to walk through life with.

Then there's connection. A connection with our church, a connection with somebody who's willing to walk along side us and give us a little advice here and there. We'd like a connection that gives us the opportunity to pour our lives out for somebody else—and that whole walk along side us thing, we're willing to do that for someone else, too.

And finally there's depth. Kiddie pools are for kids. We're looking to dive in, head first, to all the hard-to-talk-about topics, the tough questions, and heavy Scriptures. We're thinking this is a good thing, because we're in process. We're becoming. And who we're becoming isn't shallow.

We're glad you're here. Be sure and check us out online at:

THREADSMEDIA.COM

STOP BY TO JOIN OUR ONLINE COMMUNITY — AND COME BY TO VISIT OFTEN!

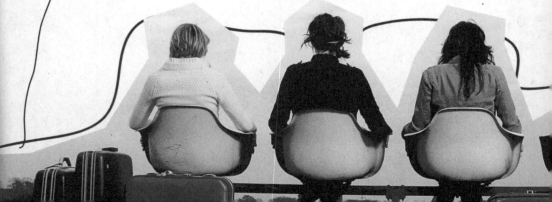

GET UNCOMFORTABLE
SERVE THE POOR. STOP INJUSTICE.
CHANGE THE WORLD … IN JESUS' NAME.
BY TODD PHILLIPS

Phillips guides you to understand how your faith in Christ and concern for the poor go hand-in-hand. As he examines God's character and perspective regarding poverty and injustice, he offers an understanding of what God calls you to do, along with practical ways to impact culture by caring for "the least of these."

TODD PHILLIPS *is the teaching pastor of Frontline, the young adult ministry of McLean Bible Church near Washington D.C. His passions are teaching the people of God and sharing the gospel with those who aren't yet Christians. He is the author of* Spiritual CPR: Reviving a Flat-lined Generation.

RED REVOLUTION
SEEING THE WORLD THROUGH THE LENS OF CHRIST
BY ADAM THOMASON

Red Revolution acknowledges that we all see the world through our own set of lenses. Those lenses color everything we see, including each other. Thomason challenges us to embrace our cultural differences, and what we have in common, in order to exalt Christ above everything else.

ADAM THOMASON *is one of the associate pastors of The Village Church, Dallas Northway campus, in addition to being the director and vision-caster for Red Revolution Adam resides in Dallas, Texas, where he and his family live out the calling of infiltrating Christ in the culture.*

SENT
LIVING THE MISSIONAL NATURE OF THE CHURCH
BY ED STETZER

Through a thorough examination of the church's call to move outside its walls, noted cultural commentator and missiologist Ed Stetzer urges Christ-followers to understand their privilege and responsibility to go into the world and take with them the transforming gospel of Jesus Christ.

ED STETZER *has planted churches in three states and trained pastors and church planters on five continents. He holds two masters degrees and two doctorates, and has written dozens of articles and books. Ed has taught at more than 15 seminaries and is currently the director of LifeWay Research and LifeWay's missiologist in residence.*

FOR FULL DETAILS ON ALL OF THREADS' STUDIES, VISIT *THREADSMEDIA.COM.*

GROUP CONTACT INFORMATION

Name _____ Number _____

E-mail _____

Name _____ Number _____

E-mail _____

Name _____ Number _____

E-mail _____

Name _____ Number _____

E-mail _____

Name _____ Number _____

E-mail _____

Name _____ Number _____

E-mail _____

Name _____ Number _____

E-mail _____

Name _____ Number _____

E-mail _____

Name _____ Number _____

E-mail _____

Name _____ Number _____

E-mail _____